# Money, Debt and Politics

This book presents an innovative history of the first Portuguese public bank, by exploring the relationship between banking activities and the political context. It provides an overview of the origins of the banking system in Portugal, and also in Brazil, and explores new archive materials related to the first years of activity of the Bank of Lisbon and to the public debates on monetary and public finance topics.

It discusses the main features of the Bank of Lisbon: a private bank with a mandate to issue banknotes for the purposes of regulating monetary circulation, and with the function of financing the State for current payments, as well as for the amortisation of public debt and the creation of new debt. The aim of contributing to the re-establishment of public trust and credit conferred upon the Bank of Lisbon the status of a quasi-central bank with the obligations of lending and issuing money.

This historical case study offers new insights for a better understanding of the role of banks on the regulation of monetary circulation and on the management of sovereign debt. By stressing the relevance of the political context, it also illustrates the key issues of trust, independence and rules associated to decision-making processes in the study of European banking history.

The main focus is the link between banking practices and the political environment. However, the reader will also engage in discussions on theoretical and economic policy issues on the main economic topics under survey: money, paper money, public debt and credit system.

**José Luís Cardoso** is Research Professor at the Institute of Social Sciences of the University of Lisbon, Portugal.

## Routledge International Studies in Money and Banking

**Central Banks in Organizational Networks**
Entangled Market Actors
*Christoph F-D. Wu*

**Responsible Finance and Digitalization**
Implications and Developments
*Edited by Panu Kalmi, Tommi Auvinen and Marko Järvenpää*

**Digital Currencies and the New Global Financial System**
*Edited by Ranjan Aneja and Robert Dygas*

**Negative Interest Rates and Financial Stability**
Lessons in Systemic Risk
*Karol Rogowicz and Małgorzata Iwanicz-Drozdowska*

**Digital Finance and the Future of the Global Financial System**
Disruption and Innovation in Financial Services
*Edited by Lech Gąsiorkiewicz and Jan Monkiewicz*

**Sovereign Debt Sustainability**
Multilateral Debt Treatment and the Credit Rating Impasse
*Daniel Cash*

**Environmental Risk Modelling in Banking**
*Edited by Magdalena Zioło*

**Money, Debt and Politics**
The Bank of Lisbon and the Portuguese Liberal Revolution of 1820
*José Luís Cardoso*

For more information about this series, please visit: www.routledge.com/Routledge-International-Studies-in-Money-and-Banking/book-series/SE0403

# Money, Debt and Politics

## The Bank of Lisbon and the Portuguese Liberal Revolution of 1820

José Luís Cardoso

Routledge
Taylor & Francis Group
LONDON AND NEW YORK

First published 2023
by Informa Law from Routledge
4 Park Square, Milton Park, Abingdon, Oxon OX14 4RN

and by Informa Law from Routledge
605 Third Avenue, New York, NY 10158

*Informa Law from Routledge is an imprint of the Taylor & Francis Group, an informa business*



*British Library Cataloguing-in-Publication Data*
A catalogue record for this book is available from the British Library

*Library of Congress Cataloging-in-Publication Data*
Names: Cardoso, José Luís, author.
Title: Money, debt and politics : the bank of Lisbon and the Portuguese liberal revolution of 1820 / José Luís Cardoso.
Description: Milton Park, Abingdon, Oxon ; New York, NY : Routledge, 2023. | Includes bibliographical references and index.
Identifiers: LCCN 2022037122 (print) | LCCN 2022037123 (ebook) | ISBN 9781032409726 (hardback) | ISBN 9781032409733 (paperback) | ISBN 9781003355625 (ebook)
Subjects: LCSH: Banco de Lisboa—History. | Banks and banking—Portugal—History—19th century. | Portugal—History—Revolution, 1820. | Economics—Portugal—History. | Economics—Brazil—History. | Banks and banking—Brazil—History—19th century.
Classification: LCC HG3200.L74 B18533 2023 (print) | LCC HG3200.L74 (ebook) | DDC 332.109469/42—dc23/eng/20220825
LC record available at https://lccn.loc.gov/2022037122
LC ebook record available at https://lccn.loc.gov/2022037123

ISBN: 978-1-032-40972-6 (hbk)
ISBN: 978-1-032-40973-3 (pbk)
ISBN: 978-1-003-35562-5 (ebk)

DOI: 10.4324/9781003355625

Typeset in Bembo
by Apex CoVantage, LLC

# Contents

# Acknowledgements

This English edition corresponds to a partial translation of a book originally published in Portuguese – *O Banco de Lisboa e a Revolução Liberal de 1820.* Lisboa: Banco de Portugal, 2021. It is the result of a research project developed at the Instituto de Ciências Sociais (ICS) of the University of Lisbon with the financial support of the Bank of Portugal. I wish to thank ICS and the Bank of Portugal for providing me with the conditions that I needed to produce this work. A special word of thanks is due to the Deputy Governor of the Bank of Portugal, Luís Máximo dos Santos, whose great enthusiasm lay at the origin of this research project and its publication in both Portuguese and English

I am also grateful for the support received from António Gil Matos and Filipe Manuel Fernandes of the Historical Archive of the Bank of Portugal, and for their help with the remote access facilities that I required for the consultation of archive materials. I also wish to thank the archivists and technical staff of the Parliamentary Historical Archive for their helpful support in the consultation of the manuscripts kept in its collections. The research assistance provided by Renato Pistola is gratefully acknowledged. A special word of thanks is due to John Elliott for the English translation of the original Portuguese version of this book (with the exception of Chapter 3).

Finally, I wish to express my gratitude to two anonymous reviewers for their careful reading of the manuscript and for their useful comments and recommendations.

***

I recently published an abridged chapter on the history of the foundation of the Bank of Lisbon, which contained references to the political context of the time: José Luís Cardoso, Money, Banking and Politics in Early Nineteenth-Century Portugal, in M.C. Marcuzzo, G. Deleplace and P. Paesani (eds.), *New Perspectives on Political Economy and its History*. London: Palgrave Masmillan, 2020, 107–125. I am grateful to the editors and publisher of this volume for their permission to use a few excerpts from this chapter in Sections 4.1., 5.4. and 5.5.

I am also grateful to CTT, Correios de Portugal (the Portuguese Post Office) for permission to reproduce, in Chapter 3 of the present book, some excerpts from the English version of José Luís Cardoso, *The Liberal Revolution of 1820*. Lisboa: CTT, 2019 (translated by José Manuel Godinho and revised by John Elliott for this edition).

# 1 Introduction

The Bank of Lisbon was founded by legal charter on 31 December 1821. Its creation was warmly welcomed and decided upon by the *Cortes Constituintes* (Parliament or Constitutional Assembly) of 1821–22, summoned following the military uprisings of 1820 (on 24 August in Porto and 15 September in Lisbon), that marked the beginning of the Portuguese Liberal Revolution.

These uprisings had a series of aims: to replace the regency that governed in the name of King João VI (who had been living in Rio de Janeiro, Brazil, since 1808, the year when the country was invaded by Napoleon's army); to demand the return of the monarch to Lisbon; and to entrust to a provisional governing body the mandate to prepare the convening of parliament in order to draft a constitution. This was the first step in the construction of a new constitutional monarchic regime in Portugal, which was to represent a decisive landmark in the evolution of Portuguese society throughout the nineteenth century. The liberal revolution of 1820 was an essential part of the contemporary history of the country, notwithstanding the defeat that it suffered in April 1823, when a counter-revolutionary coup re-established the previous absolutist order. However, after a period of political turmoil that resulted in the civil war of 1832–34, the seeds of the first liberal movement of 1820 were finally sown.

The celebration of the 200th anniversary of those decisive moments in the construction of a new political regime is a timely pretext for deepening our knowledge of the events, personalities and institutions that best characterise a historical period lived with such intensity. The creation of the Bank of Lisbon was a crucial element in a process of change and institutional innovation that shook the economic, social and political foundations of the Portuguese *ancien regime*. Its gestation was associated with the need to reorganise the process of monetary circulation and the satisfaction of the State's commitments to private creditors. These were matters that the constitutional movement considered to be of utmost importance for the rehabilitation of public credit, and for promoting a state of trust and confidence between civil society and the representative bodies of the legislative, executive and judicial powers. Given the crucial importance of such motives, the opportunity to revisit the history of the Bank of Lisbon, while also associating it with the history of the Portuguese Liberal Revolution, does not require any additional justification.

DOI: 10.4324/9781003355625-1

There have, of course, been other studies on this subject, which is a source of natural satisfaction. The pioneering work of other historians enables newcomers to the theme to feel secure as they progress in their research, knowing in what direction they will be travelling. But it is also a natural source of awkwardness for those bold enough to return to such a well-known place: what novelties can there be that still remain to be revealed?

The fascination of being a historian also includes the delight of reading through documentary sources that have already been worked upon and of reviewing the perspectives that others have constructed, with the aim of examining those same sources in a different way, of asking different questions about what one intends to investigate, believing that it is possible to bring something new to the historiographical legacy. In the case under study here, the history of the Bank of Lisbon has a number of safe and reliable interpreters whom I shall have occasion to mention throughout the book. However, I feel justified in beginning by drawing particular attention to two works that are considered essential and indispensable for anyone venturing forth into this territory.

The first one is the book on the history of the Bank of Portugal by Damião Peres, which is, in fact, entirely dedicated to the study of its predecessor, the Bank of Lisbon (Peres 1971). This was a pioneering work in its exploration of the extremely rich collection of documents at the Historical Archive of the Bank of Portugal, from which its author prepared a painstaking and rigorous account of the history of the Bank of Lisbon based on the annual reports and accounts presented by the board of directors to the bank's General Meeting and the archival documentation relating to the shareholders, the decisions taken by the bank's governing bodies, the records of deposits, mortgages and pledges, the correspondence sent and received, the issue of currency and many other important groups of documents. In this way, Damião Peres left us not only with a narrative about the most striking events in the history of the Bank of Lisbon, but also with a valuable guide to the primary sources that are of crucial importance for anyone wishing to continue his precursory work.

The second book is the history of the Bank of Portugal by Jaime Reis, who justifiably dedicated a substantial part of the book to the study of the antecedents of the Bank of Portugal, including the creation and the functioning of the Bank of Lisbon (Reis 1996, Chapter 2). Besides undertaking his own research in the archives, Jaime Reis also made use of Damião Peres' work for the construction of information series about the activities and financial performance of the Bank of Lisbon. But, in my opinion, his greatest contribution was in the way that he framed the bank's operations and functions within the troubled context of the Portuguese public finances in the first half of the nineteenth century, especially after the Civil War of 1832–34. In this sense, Jaime Reis was, above all, interested in discussing the relationship between the banking organisation and the (public and private) financial sectors, with the aim of discovering the solutions for the State's financing and for the management of the public debt system. Insofar as it was the first institution that had to deal with such problems generated by the new liberal State, the Bank of Lisbon embarked on a programme of action that, from 1846 onwards, would be taken over and pursued by the Bank of Portugal.

Faced with this acquired historiographical legacy, it was important to differentiate the research to be undertaken through the development of a new programme of investigation. Thus, the questions that I shall seek to address in this book arise from an approach that is not centred on the institutional history of the banking organisation or on economic and financial history, for which the Bank of Lisbon is a significant case study. Instead, the path of investigation that I shall follow here relates to another series of questions that complement the previously constructed knowledge, namely:

- What are the antecedents of the history of Portuguese banking or para-banking institutions that help us to understand the genesis of the Bank of Lisbon?
- What bank projects appeared in the period before the 1820 Revolution and why were they not successful?
- How do these projects and antecedents fit into the broader panorama of the history of economic ideas about themes relating to monetary theory and policy?

These questions will be answered in Chapter 2 of this book, in which I return to and expand upon subjects that have already been analysed in some of my own previously published contributions to the theme (Cardoso 1997, 2010).

Chapter 3, specially dedicated to foreign readers unfamiliar with the Portuguese political history of the period, presents a synthesis of the historical significance of the liberal revolution that took place in Portugal in 1820, seeking to answer the following questions:

- What is the importance of the Napoleonic wars for understanding the economic collapse of the Portuguese-Brazilian empire and the climate of dissatisfaction felt by the political, mercantile and military elites?
- What was the specificity of the Portuguese revolution in the broader context of revolutions that paved the way for the contemporary era?

Although this chapter is essentially intended to analyse the context of the time, I think it is also essential for understanding the approach to the Bank of Lisbon that is adopted in the following chapters. Thus, in Chapter 4, I seek to demonstrate the importance of the new political environment that existed for the public debate about the themes of monetary circulation and the public debt, showing the quantitative and qualitative significance of contributions originating from an effervescent civil society keen to find solutions for the redemption of paper money and the resolution of the sovereign debt. The questions that I shall seek to answer are:

- What was the importance of the public sphere (periodical press and published pamphlets) in raising collective awareness about the monetary and financial difficulties that the new liberal State was called upon to resolve?

- What bank projects were being proposed to the *Cortes* and what role did the Public Finance Committee play in the management of the plans that it was receiving?
- How was the final proposal for the constitution of the Bank of Lisbon discussed at the *Cortes Constituintes*? What conditions did the legislative power consider crucial for the creation of a private bank?

Finally, Chapter 5 looks at the operations and the path followed by the Bank of Lisbon between 1822 (with the beginning of its activity in August of this same year) and 1828 (in the aftermath of the convertibility crisis at the end of 1827). Although the central aim is to understand the activities of the Bank of Lisbon in the context of the three years of the new liberal and constitutional regime, before the counter-revolutionary coup in April 1823 (known as the *Vilafrancada*), it is important to address the bank's performance at a time of great social unrest, which gave rise to theoretical and political reflections on monetary and financial themes. The fundamental questions under analysis are:

- Who were the shareholders and directors of the Bank of Lisbon and what connections did they have with the economic and political agents? What was the bank's model of governance and decision-making?
- What were the main sources of the bank's profit and dividends? What was the bank's role in the financing of the State?
- What were the factors explaining the banking crisis of 1827–28 and what answers were tried out in terms of monetary theory and policy?

The book ends with a final reflection (Chapter 6) about the role of the Bank of Lisbon as a private lending institution at the service of the liberal state under construction.

As an editorial complement, the book also includes an Appendix featuring the English translation of the legal charter for the creation of the Bank of Lisbon of 31 December 1821, a document that established the principles and rules for the operation of the bank.[1]

## Note

1 Readers who are familiar with the Portuguese language should bear in mind that the Portuguese edition of the book is accompanied by an anthology of contemporary sources, relating to debates in the public sphere on issues concerning the public debt and the circulation of paper money. The anthology also includes a selection of different proposals for the creation of a bank that were submitted to the consideration of the *Cortes Constituintes* and the transcription of the parliamentary debates on the legal charter of the Bank of Lisbon. The last part of the anthology includes the most relevant contributions to the theoretical and political debates on money, credit and banking during the period 1820–28.

## References

Cardoso, José Luís, 1997. *Novos Elementos Para a História Bancária de Portugal. Projetos de Banco, 1801–1803*. Lisboa: Banco de Portugal.

Cardoso, José Luís, 2010. A new contribution to the history of the Bank of Brazil (1808–1829): chronicle of a foretold failure. *Revista Brasileira de História*, 30:59, 165–189.

Peres, Damião, 1971. *História do Banco de Portugal (1821–1846)*. Lisboa: Banco de Portugal.

Reis, Jaime, 1996. *O Banco de Portugal. Das origens a 1914*. Lisboa: Banco de Portugal, Cap. II, 71–116.

# 2 Origins and antecedents of the banking system in Portugal

## 2.1 From banking practices to bank projects

The first consistent and well-grounded attempt to create a banking institution in Portugal took place in 1797, the year when the Minister Dom Rodrigo de Sousa Coutinho presented his project for the establishment of the *Banco Nacional Brigantino*.[1] Before this project, there had been other well-known proposals made by Duarte Gomes Solis (1622) and Padre António Vieira (1646), as well as the decree issued by King João IV, which established a bank in favour of the Irish businessman Diogo Preston, destined 'for the performance of crown revenues', although this bank never entered into operation.[2]

The development of activities of a banking nature (such as money counting, deposits, loans, foreign currency transactions and the discounting of bills of exchange) had naturally increased as a result of the process of commercial expansion that Portugal had been experiencing, especially since the second half of the fifteenth century.[3] Notwithstanding the regularity of such practices, their size never made it necessary to institutionalise banks or banking services, with their own autonomy and specialisation.[4] Portugal did not keep pace with the creation of specialised banking institutions in the main European markets (Roover 1974), especially in Italy (Costabile and Neal 2018) and the Netherlands (Quinn and Roberds 2009). Although Portuguese merchants actively participated in the creation of new opportunities for the increase of long-distance trade, which required appropriate financial instruments and techniques, their involvement in the burgeoning international capital market was rather limited, especially when compared to the innovative experiments of economic and financial agents operating in London, Amsterdam or Antwerp (Neal 1990, 1–19). However, it is worth noting the role played by the Portuguese Jewish community of Amsterdam in an active stock market that was vividly commented upon and accurately analysed by one of the members of that community (Cardoso 2002).

The efforts to create banking institutions began relatively late on and were finally materialised in the form of two events of special political significance. In October 1808, the creation of the Bank of Brazil (following the transfer of the king and his court from Lisbon to Rio de Janeiro, in the context of the Napoleonic wars) and, in December 1821, the establishment of the first Portuguese

DOI: 10.4324/9781003355625-2

bank, the *Banco de Lisboa*, created by a decision of Parliament meeting after the Portuguese liberal revolution of 1820.

The fact that there were no banking institutions in Portugal and its empire before 1808 does not mean that the sort of financial transactions normally conducted through banks had not been taking place before that time. In fact, individual borrowing and lending practices conducted on a personal basis, or through private institutions that centralised lending operations, are well known and well documented (Rocha 1996). The great dispersal of these operations, in which many creditors granted a range of separate loans, made it difficult to gradually compile the information that was essential for establishing the relations of trust and confidence and the guarantees that marked the procedures that should be respected in contractual ties subject to uncertainty and risk. Such attributes were reserved for a limited number of specialists in the granting of credit, who operated predominantly in the Lisbon market.

These characteristics of the Lisbon credit market were not to be found in other European cities where such activities were more heavily concentrated in the hands of the members of social groups with greater economic resources (noble families and rich merchants). The studies that have been dedicated to this theme clearly show the difference in scale and the fragility of the credit market in Lisbon in the late eighteenth century and the first decades of the nineteenth century (Rocha 1998). The greatly reduced size of this market was naturally due to the scant demand, which meant that there was no need to develop any sizeable supply of credit to private citizens.

Despite the small size of this credit market (when compared to other European countries), historical studies based on notary records and post-mortem and orphan inventories show the extent to which manufacturers, traders and consumers were reliant on loans from private individuals to be able to pay wages, buy raw materials or goods for retail sale, meet their immediate expenses or pay debts that they had previously incurred (Rocha 1996). And they also show how large-scale traders were involved in profitable operations such as the discounting of bills of exchange and the lending of money at interest (Madureira 1994 and Pedreira 1996).

In this network of credit and finance operations before the establishment of an organised banking system, it is also important to bear in mind the role that was played by religious institutions such as the poor-relief institutions known as *Misericórdias* (Holy Houses of Mercy), brotherhoods and convents. These institutions were frequently approached by high-ranking social groups namely nobles and merchants, looking for the means to pay their current and future investment expenses (Monteiro 1992 and Amorim 2006). This involved a network of agents who shared mutual rights and obligations, arising from their simultaneous participation as debtors and creditors. The *Junta do Depósito Público* (Public Deposit Board) also dedicated itself to credit operations, resorting to the revenue from distrained or seized property that it obtained from various private judgements, especially after the reform decreed by the Pombaline legislation that expressly authorised this institution to make loans.

The creation of institutions specially dedicated to the operations of deposit-taking and financing is a subject mentioned in various opinions and *arbitrios* written in the years 1796 and 1797 by Domingos Vandelli, an Italian naturalist who had lived in Portugal since 1764.[5] His proposals for the creation of banking institutions followed two possible models.

One such model would be the 'deposit or discount banks' associated with local or regional mounts of piety commissioned to collect the funds made available by the brotherhoods, *misericórdias* and public safe-deposits (Vandelli 1796–1797, 203). Vandelli does not go into great detail or make any precise proposals about the functioning of these deposits, explaining that they should charge an interest rate of 6 per cent on credit operations, with the discount banks paying 4 per cent interest to the bank's creditors (i.e. the depositors) (Vandelli 1796–1797, 252).

The other model would be the 'circulation and mortgage' banks, the most striking example of which was the Banco di San Giorgio in Genoa (one of the first banks to be created in the Italian peninsula in the early fifteenth century). Such a solution would be a private bank, 'independent of the government', but with the primary function of attending to the needs of the State. To this end, it would collect all revenue from public contracts, the diamonds existing in the Royal Exchequer, and the capital and stocks of the extinct monopoly trading companies created during the governance of the Marquis of Pombal (between 1750 and 1777). It would also have the function of centralising the collection of the *dízimo* (the ecclesiastical tithe) and the *Quinto do Ouro* (the 'fifth of gold' tax levied on gold production), as well as the revenues from the mint, stamp-impressed paper and the postal services. In practice, therefore, it replaced the administrative departments of the Exchequer with responsibility for collecting a substantial part of the State revenues.

The counterpart of such benefits would be the obligation to advance to the State the amount of the income corresponding to such revenues. The bank would also be responsible for issuing notes to increase monetary circulation and administer the mortgages contracted for the granting of credit (to individuals and the State). Despite making only scant reference to the governance of this institution, Vandelli explicitly advocated the participation of foreigners, namely Jews, in the bank's capital, and mentioned the name of the minister Sousa Coutinho as the person best qualified to promote the organisation of this bank. However, his mistrust of the local management of the bank led him to admit the possibility of 'welcoming people from London or Amsterdam to direct this new establishment' (Vandelli 1796–1797, 382).

In some of these suggestions, Vandelli drew attention to the political and diplomatic conjuncture of the years 1796 and 1797, in which the French and Spanish threats were a factor in discouraging potential shareholders from investing their capital in high-risk financial transactions. After the opening of the first public loan of 4,000 *contos*[6] (4 billion *réis*) and the consequent issue of public debt securities, in a text dated July 1797, Vandelli expressed his concern about the difficulty of setting up a bank due to the distrust of the shareholders about receiving 'discredited paper' in exchange for the funds invested (Vandelli 1796–1797, 402).

It was certainly these difficulties and the dubious credibility of the system of public finance that explained Sousa Coutinho's inability to find the financial support necessary for his National Bank project, dated July 1797, when he was in charge of the Ministry of the Navy and Overseas Dominions. The capital of the bank would be 1,600 *contos*, distributed equally between the State and private shareholders. Under the terms of its bylaws, the bank proposed to fulfil several objectives for the issue of banknotes, the deposit of metallic money, payment advances and the discounting of bills of exchange. However, the crucial problem underlying the proposal for the bank's formation was the loan to the State of the amount necessary for the amortisation of the internal public debt, arising from the loan of 4,000 *contos* taken out in November 1796.[7]

This issuing of debt securities had been justified by the fall in crown revenues (mainly due to the decrease in tariff revenues) and by the increase in expenses associated with the Portuguese participation in the military campaigns of the Pyrenees, from 1793 to 1795, in which Portugal fought alongside the Spanish army, trying to counter the hegemonic French pretensions with respect to the Iberian Peninsula. Nonetheless, the failure to meet the deadlines for interest payments and for the amortisation of debt securities led to feelings of distrust regarding the credibility of the public authorities. And, of course, it removed authority or moral value from any political action that the State wished to promote in other areas of financial and fiscal administration.

Thus, the proposal for the constitution of the National Bank had the fundamental goal of serving as a means for financing the State, the aim being to meet the burdens arising from the public debt contracted through the loan of November 1796. It was also the same purpose that was presented in another project, based on Sousa Coutinho's plan, which circulated in the form of a flyer in the year 1800, although nothing resulted from this (*Plano* 1800).[8]

Sousa Coutinho's banking solution was designed to make the State appear credible and to reassure public opinion regarding the process of public debt management. However, what prevailed was another solution linked to the issue of new debt securities of a very low nominal value (small *apólices*). These bonds began to circulate as inconvertible paper money and, due to their uncontrolled and fraudulent issue, caused inflationary effects and disturbances to the monetary circulation.[9] As we shall see later on, it was the negative consequences of this issue of paper money – which replaced the previous bonds (*apólices*) that were supposed to serve as debt securities and whose discounting resulted in huge losses for their owners (about 25 per cent of the initial value) – that lay behind the creation of the Bank of Lisbon in 1821.[10]

The failure to implement Sousa Coutinho's project was certainly due to the lack of commitment on the part of the rich merchants who had been contacted for this purpose. The initiative of creating a bank did not merit their consideration, certainly because they could not expect it to provide them with profitable capital investment. This also meant that, as far as the performance of their own business was concerned, credit practices were carried out through an informal structure of bank-like operations exercised by the agents themselves and the chambers of commerce, namely payment delays and deferrals, and the issue of bills of exchange, as well as through personal borrowing operations at low interest rates (Pedreira 1996). As already pointed out, the same thing happened in situations of lesser economic impact, but perhaps with greater social significance, which involved daily credit operations conducted among low-income social groups. Thus, at the dawn of the nineteenth century, economic activities took place in Portugal with the aid of parabanking instruments, but without an institution specifically conceived for this purpose.

There were, however, indications that some advantages were to be gained by institutionalising banking practices, for two fundamental reasons.

In the first place, this would be the most appropriate way of quelling the rumours and suspicions about the legitimacy of procedures that the country's persistent and retrograde traditions continued to classify as usury. Only in this way can we explain how, just under two decades before the end of the eighteenth century, there still continued to be heated discussions about the licit nature of charging interest. Such debate involved arguments from the perspective of divine and moral law, as well as criteria of economic rationality, in order to appease the more scrupulous consciences that exercised greater vigilance in relation to the legitimacy of their economic activities.[11]

The existence of autonomous banking institutions would also be useful for a second reason: it would allow for the establishment of regular and more fluid relations between the productive and trading sectors and the services that banks would be required to provide, which entailed more resources and a greater technical capacity, thus revealing the need for greater specialisation.

During the period under analysis – in other words, in the late eighteenth and early nineteenth centuries – this was the background to the presentation of several projects for the formation of banks whose functions did not expressly involve the specific needs of financing the State, managing the public debt or reorganising the circulation of paper money. Their objective would, above all, be to support the development of economic activities and to serve the private economic agents.

This different typology applied to three bank projects sent to Dom Rodrigo de Sousa Coutinho, from 1801 to 1803. This period corresponded precisely to his term of service as President of the Royal Exchequer, which represented a crucial moment in the political and financial management that he sought to bring to the realm's business dealings. The origin of these projects is consequently automatically explained by the political importance of the person to whom they were addressed.[12] Given his prominent position in the Prince Regent's office, and given his special vocation for dealing with matters relating to the organisation of the State's financial structure, Sousa Coutinho was the privileged interlocutor of those who, acting either on their own initiative or in fulfilment of the wishes of others, sought to put into practice innovative ideas in relation to economic or financial matters. The sending of such proposals sometimes also corresponded to requests made by the President of the Royal Exchequer himself, who, in this way, sought to obtain the suggestions and opinions of advisers or friends who were specifically qualified to provide them.[13]

The first proposal for a bank was presented to Dom Rodrigo de Sousa Coutinho by Feliciano António Nogueira in 1801 and was entitled *Plano para formar um Banco Nacional* (Plan for the Formation of a National Bank). Its author presented the customary provisions relating to the founding capital, the number of shares and the form for their public subscription, as well as the corresponding 5 per cent interest rate. He also specified the bank's main responsibilities – discounting bills of exchange and advancing funds to its clients, both of which operations would provide the bank with 6 per cent interest – and explained the form for the State's participation in the bank's capital. In concrete terms, this would consist of subscribing to 1/4 of the total capital of 3,200 *contos* by depositing the corresponding amount in the form of rough diamonds.[14] The plan also contemplated other organisational aspects relating to the administration and management of the bank. The most interesting aspects of this plan were the ones that related, first, to the definition of its privileged vocation for granting credit to agriculture (also at 6 per cent interest). Second, to the request that was made in return for the bank to be able to promote the business of white textiles from Bengal under a system of exclusive privilege for an 80-year period. Was this benefit considered to be excessive in view of the limited advantages that the State could enjoy through the sale of the diamonds? We now know that the project was never followed through, becoming lost amid the archived dossiers of its recipient.

A further point of interest in Feliciano António Nogueira's plan was the understanding that it showed about the economic advantages of increasing the velocity of monetary circulation and the care with which he advocated the mandatory convertibility of paper money into specie. 'Banknotes and metallic money will be considered to be of equal value, since all of the bank's credit will be established in the honour that must be paid to its notes, as soon as these are presented to it'. This convertibility was a central question, so that the virtues of monetary circulation could be kept intact when this was conducted through the use of paper money.

As far as the intention to grant priority credit to the agricultural sector is concerned, there was an obvious link to other programmes and instruments designed to support the development of agriculture, which also afforded access to funds at privileged interest rates. This was the express or implied intention of projects for the establishment of local and regional economic societies that, without having the power or reach of their counterparts in Spain at that time – the *Sociedades Económicas de Amigos del País* – which were spreading rapidly across the whole country, were nonetheless designed to bring together social interests, increase technical skills and afford access to capital funds. All of these aspects were considered to be essential conditions for the much-desired development of the country's agricultural sector. In this particular context, the plan presented by an anonymous author should be highlighted, as it proposed the creation of agricultural *montepios* (mounts of piety) that would provide interest-free credit during the first year of the loan, with the respective capital being raised through the payment of a slight tax (1–2 per cent) on the value of crops and the transactions of products. The guarantees for this type of loan would be provided through the mortgaging of properties or through the deposit of silver or gold objects (*Plano* 1781).

A second plan presented to Dom Rodrigo de Sousa Coutinho had the name of *Banco de Empréstimo sobre Penhores* (Bank of Pledged Loans), and it was drawn up in 1803 by João Henriques Sequeira, an official at the Office of the Secretary of State for Foreign Affairs and War. Despite the limited range of activity that was planned for this bank, it clearly reveals the significance that small short-term loans had in the Portuguese economy of that time. The fundamental aim announced by the author of the plan was to forestall usurious practices that would penalise the members of underprivileged social groups or those who had suffered an unexpected fall in revenue, in order to 'avoid many lending operations, torments and sacrifices, and consequently many ruins'. Technical rules and estimations of costs were factors that were included in this project introduced through a letter of presentation in which the author requested compensations in return. He would later repeat his proposal on two more occasions in 1819 and 1821, accompanied by a request for benefits in an identical plan for the creation of an institution geared towards the practice of pledges and mortgages.[15]

The third and last project, presented by Henrique Palyart de Clamouse and dated 1802, proposed the foundation of a *Banco de Portugal estabelecido em Lisboa* (Bank of Portugal established in Lisbon). This document is highly important for the study of the precursory proposals for the creation of a bank in Portugal.

Henrique Palyart divided his plan into two parts: the bank's conditions towards the public and the rules to be established among the respective shareholders. As far as the first aspect was concerned, he presented the bank's aims and functions, namely the discounting of bills of exchange, promissory notes and paper money; advances of funds against the value of securities awaiting clearance; deposits, collections, payments, transfers and applications of funds; and the issue and circulation of banknotes. In all of these operations, the bank would collect or pay the respective interest fixed by law, maintaining complete secrecy and reserving the right not to perform any operations that might be suspected of being unlawful.

As far as the second part of the plan was concerned, Henrique Palyart referred to the conditions for subscribing to the bank's capital (4,800 *contos*), corresponding to 10,000 shares of 480$000 – of which only 1/10 would be used as initial capital, with the remainder being converted into banknotes issued in order to circulate as money. The subscription would be made in equal parts by 10 'interested' businessmen, whose names were listed in a note annexed to the bank project. Under the clauses of this project, provisions were made for the various technical procedures relating to subscriptions, endorsements and transactions among the shareholders, who would automatically constitute the bank's board of directors on a lifetime basis. The three executive directors would be chosen by lot from among the ten shareholders for specific periods of time, which clearly revealed their united purposes and the relationship of mutual trust that existed between the bank's promoters, all of whom belonged to the Portuguese commercial and financial oligarchy at the beginning of the nineteenth century. In fact, in the list of subscribers that was included at the end of the plan, we can find the names of important families of traders on the Lisbon market, such as Cruz Sobral, Caldas, Machado, Vanzeller and Palyart.[16]

In a signed note on the front page of this bank proposal, Dom Rodrigo de Sousa Coutinho wrote that 'this project is unworthy of attention'. Why was it rejected, given that, five years earlier, Sousa Coutinho had himself envisaged the participation of businessmen as subscribers to his own National Bank? We consider it plausible to put forward two arguments justifying the rejection of the proposal, taking into account the characteristics and the nature of both bank projects. In the first place, it seems perfectly reasonable that the President of the Royal Exchequer would not find it convenient to restrict the number of people interested in subscribing to the bank's capital to ten, which would mean reducing the scope of its effects among the social group sponsoring the bank's formation.[17] Or, in other words, regardless of the fact that this was an initiative that did not contemplate the participation of the State as a shareholder, it was a restricted society of businessmen who were certainly seeking to promote their own interests. Second, it also seems plausible to consider that, in the view of Dom Rodrigo de Sousa Coutinho, the bank did not meet the essential requirement with which it had drawn up its project, namely that of enabling the effective financing of the State with a view to meeting the charges of the public debt.

Although Henrique Palyart's proposal contained a reference to operations for the discounting of paper money, this activity did not take place under the unequivocal understanding that it would be the bank's mission to serve as the State's creditor. It was perhaps for this reason, the author of the plan sought new elements to justify the virtues of his project, seemingly wishing to adapt some of its aims in order to satisfy the expectations that the President of the Royal Exchequer would have in relation to the public function that was to be performed by a private banking institution. This is what is revealed to us through the reading of some additional documents written by Henrique Palyart, which were annexed to his bank project in the form of appendices.

In the first of those texts, *Benefícios que podem resultar de um banco nacional* (Benefits that may result from a national bank), Henrique Palyart's argument is based precisely on the possibility of the provision of a loan to the State, together with the advantages associated with the creation of a commercial company promoted by the bank. With this dual idea, he showed that he was, to some extent, influenced by the experiences in France of the famous bank developed by Law, which did, in fact, merit some treatment and autonomous praise in the second appendix to the proposal, entitled *Nota do benefício que pode fazer um banco a um Estado* (Note on the benefits that a bank may bring to a State). At a time when John Law's financial activities were normally regarded as an easy target for attacks against the risks of fiduciary money, Henrique Palyart preferred to extol the virtues of accelerating the circulation of money, when such a process was carefully controlled and managed.[18] Finally, the third appendix, *Ideias gerais sobre a importância das caixas de desconto* (General ideas about the importance of discount houses), presented a well-constructed argument about the role of banks and credit as factors leading to an increase in the volume of transactions and an expansion of productive activities.

One final project related to the creation of a bank that Sousa Coutinho had idealised in the years 1802 and 1803 involved the foreign banking houses of Baring Brothers & Company, of London, and Hope & Cia, of Amsterdam. This project was a by-product of the relationship between the Portuguese State and the banking houses serving as intermediaries for the heavy indemnity that Portugal was forced to pay to France in the aftermath of the Peace Treaties of Badajoz and Madrid, signed in 1801 after the Portuguese defeat by the French-Spanish coalition. For the payment of the war indemnity, Portugal agreed a loan of 4,000 *contos* with these leading European merchant bankers, which was facilitated by their offering as collateral the sales value of diamonds from Brazil, equivalent to half the value of the loan. Notwithstanding the good relationship between Sousa Coutinho and Pierre-César Labouchère, the representative sent to Lisbon by Baring & Hope, the latter's participation in the capital of a bank did not take place.[19]

## 2.2 In search of a theoretical framework

Although they were never realised, when taken together, these different proposals for the creation of banking institutions offer a very significant testimony to the monetary and financial problems that were under debate in Portugal in the early years of the nineteenth century. They consequently provide us with a more rigorous reflection upon the type of solutions that would later be encountered in the debates on the creation of the Bank of Lisbon in the new political environment resulting from the liberal revolution of 1820.

It should, however, be emphasised that the theoretical framework of bank projects viewed in the light of the teachings of political economy was certainly not one of the most important features of those projects that were narrowly disseminated in the early years of the nineteenth century. José Acúrsio das Neves was one of the few authors who, in the period before the liberal revolution of 1820, discussed the problems of banking organisation, based on the arguments and principles of political economy.

In the chapter that he devoted to 'considerations on public credit, paper money and bank operations' (Neves 1814–1817, 403–471), Acúrsio das Neves set out his views on the need to ensure a financial system based on principles of mutual trust which form the basis of the credibility between public and private actors establishing formal contractual relations. In other words, credit operations and contracts presuppose the reliability of, and trust among, the participants:

> When governments set the example of good faith and correctness in fulfilling their obligations, when they identify their fortune with that of private individuals, credit operations are greatly facilitated, and everything contributes to the common good.
>
> (Neves 1814–1817, 408)

The maintenance of an atmosphere of trust and creditworthiness presupposed the need to constantly consolidate the existing public debt. Therefore, taking care of the allocation of the funds needed for the payment of debt interest and the amortisation of the capital that had been lent would be the first step towards reassuring creditors about the State's compliance with its obligations.

Acúrsio das Neves had no doubts about the advantages of a public debt system through which the wealth amassed by private individuals could improve the circulation of money, obtaining increased profitability on their stock of capital and contributing to the funding of State expenditures. However, he considered it essential to prevent the risk of abuses and the accumulation of State debts without any justification of the public service that should result from such indebtedness. Looking for arguments to sustain his thoughts on the subject, Neves resorted to the authority of authors like J.-B. Say, G. Filangieri, J. Necker and S. Sismondi.

Besides the public debt instrument, it seemed plausible to him that State spending could be financed through taxation, in particular through an income tax, similar to the one that had been introduced in England by William Pitt in 1797. And also through the rationalisation, simplification and regulation of the tax collection system.

Acúrsio das Neves presented the wide range of different forms that existed for the circulation of paper money, in order to establish a clear distinction between the convertible banknotes, which were used as money and complemented the circulation of specie, and the debt securities and credit paper issued by the State (*apólices*) or by private individuals (bills of exchange and land bills). The latter were not intended to be used as currency, but were technical instruments placed at the service of the expansion of productive and mercantile activities, provided that they were carefully managed.

In making this basic distinction, Acúrsio das Neves accounted for the risks associated with the overissue of paper money, without taking into account the desired proportion that should be maintained, whether between the paper issued and the capital of the issuing institution, or between the quantity of money (specie and paper) in circulation and the annual wealth produced. His concern was to warn of the negative consequences of an excess of paper money circulating in Portugal, using the approaches of Adam Smith and J.-B. Say, who recommended prudence and control over the quantity issued, taking into account the level of wealth created and represented.

It therefore seems useful to briefly recall Adam Smith's position on the advantages and disadvantages of fiduciary circulation. For the author of the *Wealth of Nations*, the circulation of consumer goods could be accelerated through the smooth functioning of the monetary sphere, which could accommodate the issue of paper money:

> The substitution of paper in the room of gold and silver money, replaces a very expensive instrument of commerce with one much less costly, and sometimes equally convenient. Circulation comes to be carried on by a new wheel, which it costs less both to erect and to maintain than the old one.
>
> (Smith 1776, II. ii, 292)

The advantages of the 'new wheel', or, in other words, of paper money, were twofold: on the one hand, it brought an increase in the velocity of circulation of specie and the consequent diminution of its proportionality vis-à-vis the domestic product that it was supposed to represent; on the other hand, it meant the conversion of a portion of inactive capital into active and productive capital through the indispensable banking operations that would necessarily accompany the substitution of gold and silver by paper money. In either of these areas, the fundamental question underlying them is the possibility that the specie removed from circulation will become a productive investment fund. In this way, Smith revealed some sensitivity to the function of money as a factor of value creation, drawing closer to David Hume's theses about the non-neutrality and expansionist effects of money during the time elapsing between the flow of specie and its repercussions on the level of prices.

However, in other more abundant passages of his work, Smith offers us counter arguments that point to the element of undisguised insecurity inherent in an increase in fiduciary circulation. In the highly suggestive words of the author of the *Wealth of Nations*:

> The gold and silver money which circulates in any country may very properly be compared to a highway, which, while it circulates and carries to market all the grass and corn of the country, produces itself not a single pile of either. The judicious operations of banking, by providing, if I may be allowed so violent a metaphor, a sort of waggon-way through the air; enable the country to convert, as it were, a great part of its highways into good pastures and corn fields, and thereby to increase very considerably the annual produce of its land and labour. The commerce and industry of the country, however, it must be acknowledged, though they may be somewhat augmented, cannot be altogether so secure, when they are thus, as it were, suspended upon the Daedalian wings of paper money, as when they travel about upon the solid ground of gold and silver. Over and above the accidents to which they are exposed from the unskilfulness of

> the conductors of this paper money, they are liable to several others, from which no prudence or skill of those conductors can guard them.
>
> (Smith 1776, II. ii, 321)

Daedalus' wings and the possibility of travel accidents along the way called for precautions. The first precaution would be to control the issue of paper money in such a way that the total amount of this in circulation did not exceed the corresponding value of gold and silver. This postulate implies another indispensable condition to guarantee the solidity of the fiduciary circulation system, in order to prevent its inflationary effects: the convertibility of paper money into specie.[20]

Thus, with Adam Smith's solid endorsement, we once again encounter José Acúrsio das Neves' concerns when he points to the need for the wheel of circulation to correctly fulfil its economic function. It is in this sense that he discusses the feasibility and opportunity of creating a bank or discount house with the mission of regularising the amortisation of public debt and the circulation of paper money, recalling the failed experiments that had taken place since Sousa Coutinho had proposed his plan for a National Bank in 1797.

The theme also served as a pretext for Acúrsio das Neves to undertake a brief survey of the processes that had been followed in setting up the main European banks, namely in Austria, England, France, Hamburg, Italy (Padua, Genoa, Venice and Naples) and Spain, explaining their distinct vocation: in some cases, they had the priority objectives of withdrawing inconvertible paper money from circulation and managing the public debt system (Austria, England and Spain); in other cases, their purpose was to take deposits and make loans and advances (France, Italy and Prussia), with the aim of fostering the development of agriculture and manufacturing sectors. He also paid special attention to the case of savings banks, which were designed to capture significant amounts of small private savings and could play an important role in boosting investment in productive economic sectors.

The panorama presented by Acúrsio das Neves anticipated and heralded the discussion about the need for a banking institution in Portugal that was to occur after the liberal revolution of 1820. When Acúrsio das Neves published his book *Variedades*, the Bank of Brazil was already in operation, to which he made a short reference. The specificity of its creation justifies our providing a brief overview of the fundamental features of this pioneering institution.

## 2.3 The Bank of Brazil (1808)

The Bank of Brazil had been established by charter in Rio de Janeiro on 12 October 1808 and was part of the set of economic and financial measures naturally associated with the transfer of the Portuguese court to Brazil, following the invasion of continental Portugal in November 1807 by Napoleon's forces under the command of Junot.[21] Those measures included the inaugural Royal

Charter of 28 January 1808, which established new rules opening Brazilian ports to international trade, the new legislative framework accepting the installation of manufactures in Brazil (1 April 1808) and the creation or adaptation of royal institutions – such as the Board of Trade or the Royal Exchequer – to the new political environment resulting from the court's expected lengthy stay in Rio de Janeiro. These were some of the principal political actions that enable us to understand the urgent need for the creation of a banking and financial instrument with the aim of organising and centralising the indispensable operations of monetary circulation, as well as financing public and private economic activities).

The lack of specie in circulation, or, in other words, the excessive demand for money due to the opening of the ports and the consequent increase in transactions, which were, in turn, related to the increase in public services and the greater expenditure involved in establishing the court in Brazil, were all factors that justified the devising of new solutions designed to facilitate the creation and circulation of money.

The foundation of the Bank of Brazil was certainly encouraged and promoted by Sousa Coutinho, who, although he did not exercise any formal supervision over this area of governance, had a proverbial fondness for matters relating to financial organisation and administration. As discussed earlier, both the project that he had conceived in 1797 and the plans that were addressed to him between 1801 and 1803 were mainly concerned with regularising the circulation of paper money and with the management of the public debt system. In Rio de Janeiro, in 1808, the dominant concerns and intentions were different, which is clearly visible in the aims outlined in the charter that created the Bank of Brazil and that served as the preamble for its regulatory articles of association.

The foundation of the Bank of Brazil was motivated by the lack of funds available to the Royal Exchequer, the need to create more efficient means of payment, and also the need to remove obstacles to the development of trade deals (*Alvará*, 12 October 1808).[22] Therefore, the Bank of Brazil was designed with a triple function of guaranteeing improvements in the funding of the State ('to facilitate access to the means and resources that my royal and public revenues need to meet the State's expenses'), in monetary circulation ('to activate the accounts not being used, in both commercial goods and minted specie'), and in productive investment ('to promote national industry through the combination and circulation of isolated capital').

This was an extremely ambitious programme, with some of these good intentions being achieved in the way in which the bank's articles of association (article VII) systematically organised deposits, loans and the issue of paper money, all of which were operations that the bank was authorised to perform. Among the privileges given to the bank were the management of exclusive contracts for diamonds, brazilwood, ivory and cudbear. However, it was possible to foresee that certain difficulties lay ahead in the fulfilment of its mission, such as the way in which the capital of the new bank would be attracted and subscribed, the form that was conceived for its administrative structure, the non-definition of questions relating to the links between the bank's private capital and the management of public funds by the Royal Exchequer, as well as the absence of any rules or restrictions placed on the issue of paper money.

An integrated vision of this set of operations was presented by José da Silva Lisboa, shortly after the formal establishment of the Bank of Brazil:

> However, to guard against the misappropriation of royal rights, facilitate payments and overcome a lack of ready cash, which the emergencies of war or the circumstances of trade might require, His Royal Highness has ordered expedients and regulations for this purpose, creating a royal bank; which, being well administered, as in England, is equivalent to rich mines. It is the Potosi of immense wealth; since it will give the nation inexhaustible public credit to turn all of the pecuniary capitals, which previously had been dead and unproductive due to their lack of useful employment, into profitable assets.
>
> (Lisboa 1810, 451)

The new bank's mission was praised for adopting a broader doctrinal framework in relation to the advantages of free trade and for streamlining the instruments of monetary circulation, as can be clearly seen in the following passage:

> When the exchange and discount operations are better known and appreciated, with the progress of public credit and the greater knowledge of trade, when all senseless fear ceases and people properly understand the convenience of letting our gold leave the country to be employed in more profitable business abroad, then perhaps banknotes will become the most common currency and the great instruments and vehicle of circulation.
>
> (Lisboa 1810, 451)

It is interesting to note that both Dom Rodrigo de Sousa Coutinho's 1797 project for the *Banco Real Brigantino* and Henrique Palyart's 1802 project for the Bank of Portugal contained lists of businessmen who might subscribe to the capital of these banks.[23] The same care of previously identifying potential capitalists does not seem to have been taken in the case of the creation of the Bank of Brazil, which may serve to explain the 1-year delay in obtaining the subscription of the minimum number of shares needed for the bank's launch. It should also be noted that the founding capital of 1,200 *contos* (divided into 1,200 shares of 1,000$00 each) would only be reached 10 years after the creation of the Bank of Brazil.

One aspect that is worthy of special mention is the novelty that was introduced into the organisational structure of a company limited by shares, as was the case with the Bank of Brazil, which was endowed with limited liability (article III of its articles of association), namely the setting up of a reserve fund amounting to a sixth of the value of the subscribed shares (article XIX) and the creation of an administrative model that did away with the practice that was current at that time in companies limited by shares. This new model was based on the existence of a general meeting restricted to the 40 largest shareholders who had the power to appoint a board with ten members and a management committee with four members (articles IX and X).[24]

Start-up difficulties led to major changes in the bank's way of operating, embodied in the legislation approved in August and October 1812. The entry of the Royal Exchequer into the capital of the bank, through a fund originating from new taxes levied on consumer goods and which had been specially created for this purpose, as well as the granting of graces and favours to the new subscribers willing to risk their capital, were measures that brought a new lease of life to the institution and enabled it to respond positively to the increasing needs resulting from the greater confidence and enthusiasm of the national and foreign traders operating in the Rio de Janeiro market.

This new impulse given to the Bank of Brazil boosted its activity as an issuing bank, especially from 1814 onwards, when the quantity of paper money in circulation increased drastically, despite the fact that there were no supervisory means or instruments of control in existence to prevent the risks inherent in the increase in fiduciary circulation. In fact, besides there being no statutory provisions for controlling the issues of paper money, such issues were made without taking into account the demands of the market and the metallic funds that would be needed to serve as their guarantee. The basic principle of limiting the ratio between the banknotes in circulation and their metallic support, in other words the existence of funds that could be given in exchange for the paper money presented for discount purposes, was not even minimally respected. Above all, there was no inspection process or public scrutiny of the bank's public acts; in particular there was no regular publication of reports of its activities and accounts.

Besides serving as a vehicle for accelerating the court's expenditure, the issue of paper money also served as an expedient for the public works of construction in which the Bank of Brazil was involved. This status as a source of funds for the government to meet current expenditures and finance its larger-scale public projects justified the privileges that the bank demanded in terms of tax collection and the legally enforced repayment of bad debts (*Alvará* of 24 September 1814). And, when such a prerogative was not respected, due to the pressure that debtors brought to bear on the government and at the court, it was the Board of the Bank itself that recalled the successive payments of financial support from the Bank to the Royal Exchequer, amounting to an annual sum of between 5 million and 6 million *cruzados* (2,000–2,400 *contos de réis*), and threatened to reduce its contributions towards the payment of the Exchequer's commitments, as well as to change the conditions for the granting of credit to private individuals.

The demands presented by the bank's management do not conceal its excessive dependence on the Royal Exchequer and on other bodies of economic and financial organisation. The situation was consensually diagnosed as an obvious sign of the failure to perform the functions that had been entrusted to it. The revenues obtained from the management of the exclusive contracts for diamonds and brazilwood, ivory from Angola and cudbear from Cape Verde were irregular and the practice of smuggling could not be prevented. The creation of branches in São Paulo, Bahia and Minas Gerais did not have the desired effect. The increases of capital and the continuous issue of paper money were easy expedients for responding to the problems that the bank itself was creating.

At the beginning of March 1821, the crisis faced by the bank was explicitly highlighted in a decree creating a commission that was to analyse the situation and find solutions to the difficulties of the Bank of Brazil. Bearing in mind that the quantity of paper money issued in that year was more than three times the amount of the bank's capital, it was no wonder that there should be some concern about the bank's state of insolvency. Moreover, the impossibility of complying with possible requests to exchange or redeem paper money was obvious due to the irrecoverable debt of the Royal Exchequer, which had reached an amount of roughly 4,800,000$000, or, in other words, around twice the bank's capital.

The recognition of the seriousness of the situation was confirmed by the Decree of 23 March 1821, which assumed the bank's liabilities as national debt, since it had resulted from loans made to finance public spending, with the commitment of the Royal Exchequer being given as a guarantee through (the promise of) the delivery of diamonds and jewels to pay off these debts. A few days later, the decision was taken to seek a foreign loan in favour of the Bank of Brazil. When King João VI and his court returned to Lisbon on 26 April 1821 – 13 years after their triumphant arrival in Rio de Janeiro – the generous gestures for the rehabilitation of the Bank of Brazil were thwarted and invalidated, since the bank suddenly found itself stripped of the metallic funds and precious goods in its safekeeping. From then on, the bank's endemic difficulties could not be resolved and, even after the independence of Brazil in 1822, it continued to pursue solutions of indebtedness and the issue of paper money, naturally leading to its decline and to the inevitable insolvency of the institution which no longer served as a support for the banking and financial organisation of Brazil. The Bank of Brazil was officially closed in 1829.

## Notes

1 Published for the first time in Macedo 1963. A recent edition of this project, in which some of the mistakes of transcription have been corrected, is available in Coutinho 1797 [1993].

2 Reproduced in Amzalak 1919. For a general overview of the early origins of the banking history in Portugal, cf. Peres 1971 and Soares 1971.

3 On the use of credit instruments and, in general, on the practices of a banking nature that took place in Portugal during this period, cf. Almeida 1993 and Barata 1996. See also the example of the foreign exchange activity established in 1465 by Rafael Vivas, in Farinha 1992.

4 It should, however, be noted that brokerage activities, the practices of mediating business deals on the Lisbon market, had already been institutionalised, particularly from the early sixteenth century onwards. On this subject, cf. Justino 1994, 11–52.

5 Vandelli played a major role in the enlightened reform of the University of Coimbra in 1772 and the creation of the Royal Academy of Sciences in Lisbon, in 1779. He was one of the most important contributors to Portuguese economic and financial thought in the late eighteenth century (Cardoso 1990).

6 Around 1800, 1 *conto* = 1 million *réis* = £275 sterling (source: Reis 1836, 22–23).

7 This amount corresponds to roughly half of the annual average revenue of the Portuguese Exchequer throughout the period from 1797 to 1803 (Costa 2016, 606).

8 It should be mentioned that, under the aegis of Dom Rodrigo de Sousa Coutinho, experiments were also made to amortise paper money through the establishment of a Discount House (1799) and through the mission entrusted to the *Junta dos Juros* (Board of Interest) for this purpose in 1803. In a similar fashion, neither of these attempts met with any success.

9 This theme has received attention and debate in Portuguese historiography. For an overview, see Godinho 1955, Silveira 1987, Cardoso 1989, Madureira 1994 and Costa 2016.

10 Cf. Costa 1992, 58–62 and Justino 1994, 65–68. On the effects of the crisis on the structure of public finance, see Silveira 1987. On the way in which such a crisis had been inherited by the modern liberal state, see Pinheiro 1991, 8–13.

11 Favourable opinions about the legitimacy of charging interest were expressed by Braga 1784 and Sousa 1786. The defence's arguments were refuted by Ribeiro 1787.

12 About the contents of these projects for the creation of a bank and the context in which they were written, including their complete transcription, cf. Cardoso 1997.

13 It was also at Sousa Coutinho's instigation that, in 1801, the Portuguese translation was published of a brief history of the Bank of England (Fortune 1801), the purpose of which was obviously to inform public opinion about the advantages of creating a similar institution in Portugal.

14 The *Plano para a ereção de um Banco Real em Lisboa* (General Plan for the Erection of a Royal Bank in Lisbon – *Plano* 1800) also included an identical form for the participation of the Royal Exchequer in the capital of the bank that was to be set up.

15 This other project, proposed by João Henriques Sequeira and dated 1819, with the title of *Banco de Socorro ou de Empréstimo sobre Penhores* (the Support Bank or the Bank of Pledged Loans), was published in Macedo 1963, 57–74. With only slight differences, and taking the new political situation into account, the same project was submitted for the appreciation of two committees of the *Cortes Constituintes* in 1821, as we shall see later on. Also published in Macedo 1963, 37–55, was the proposal presented to the Board of Trade by the merchant João Fletcher in June 1815, which was favourably approved in relation to its proposed aims (the discounting of bills of exchange, issue of banknotes, pledged loans), but was negatively assessed by the members of the Board of Trade (including José Acúrsio das Neves) who were called upon to express their opinion, because of the exorbitant nature of the benefits and privileges requested by its proposer.

16 For more information about the main representatives of the business elite operating in Lisbon during this period, see Pedreira 1995, especially Chapter II, 125–190.

17 The number of businessmen presented by Dom Rodrigo de Sousa Coutinho as potential shareholders of the *Banco Nacional Brigantino* rose to 83 in total, some of whom were representatives of companies.

18 It is interesting to note the great praise that this Portuguese author heaped on the merits of Law's system. On the nature and relevance of Law's financial experiments, see Murphy 1997 and Velde 2009.

19 For a summary of this interesting financial episode, see Neal 2021. For a detailed report, see Buist 1974, Chapter 14 (The Portuguese Diamond Loan),

20 For an overview of Smith's position on the role of banks in the monetary system, see Gherity 1994.

21 The analysis included in this section is an abridged version of an essay dedicated to the history of the Bank of Brazil in the period 1808–29 (Cardoso 2010), in which the reader

will find all the sources and references relating to its justification and interpretation. See, also, Marcos 2014.

22 The legislation referred to here was consulted in the *Coleção das Leis do Império do Brasil* (Collection of the Laws of the Brazilian Empire), available at: http://www2.camara.gov.br/legislacao/publicacoes/doimperio

23 On the shareholders of the Bank of Brazil and their socio-economic profile, particularly those businessmen that were involved in the slave trade, see Aidar 2018.

24 On the innovative aspects of this corporate model, see Marcos 2008, 62–63.

## References


Aidar, Bruno, 2018. Financiar o império: o Banco do Brasil e seus acionistas, 1808–1821. *Working Paper, Instituto Mora*. México.

Almeida, António Marques, 1993. *Capitais e Capitalistas no Comércio da Especiaria*. Lisboa: Cosmos.

Amorim, Inês, 2006. Património e crédito: Misericórdia e Carmelitas de Aveiro (séculos XVII e XVIII). *Análise Social*, nº 180, 41:4, 693–729.

Amzalak, Moses A., 1919. *O Banco de Lisboa*. Lisboa: Instituto Superior de Comércio de Lisboa.

Barata, Filipe Themudo, 1996. Negócios e crédito: complexidade e flexibilidade das práticas creditícias /século XV). *Análise Social*, nº 136/137, 31:2/3, 683–709.

Buist, Marten G., 1974. *At Spes Non Fracta. Hope & Co. 1770–1815. Merchant Bankers and Diplomats at Work* (Chapter 14: The Portuguese Diamond Loan). The Hague: Martinus Nijhoff.

Cardoso, José Luís, 1989. *O Pensamento Económico em Portugal nos Finais do Século XVIII (1780–1808)*. Lisboa: Editorial Estampa.

Cardoso, José Luís, 1990. Economic thought in late eighteenth-century Portugal: physiocratic and Smithian influences. *History of Political Economy*, 22:3, 429–441.

Cardoso, José Luís, 1997. *Novos Elementos Para a História Bancária de Portugal. Projetos de Banco, 1801–1803*. Lisboa: Banco de Portugal.

Cardoso, José Luís, 2002. *Confusion de confusiones*: Ethics and options in seventeenth-century stock exchange markets. *Financial History Review*, 9:2, 109–123.

Cardoso, José Luís, 2010. A new contribution to the history of the Bank of Brazil (1808–1829): chronicle of a foretold failure. *Revista Brasileira de História*, 30:59, 165–189.

*Coleção das Leis do Império do Brasil* (Collection of the Laws of the Brazilian Empire), available at: http://www2.camara.gov.br/legislacao/publicacoes/doimperio

Costa, Fernando Dores, 1992. *Crise financeira, dívida pública e capitalistas (1796–1807)*. Lisboa: FCSH/UNL (dissertação mimeo).

Costa, Fernando Dores, 2016. A "nova dívida" – 1796–1803. A difusão de uma nova política financeira. *Análise Social*, nº 220, 51:3, 598–627.

Costabile, Lilia and Neal, Larry (eds.), 2018. *Financial Innovation and Resilience. A Comparative Perspective on the Public Banks of Naples (1462–1808)*. Cham: Palgrave Macmillan.

Coutinho, D. Rodrigo de Sousa, 1797. Projeto de Banco Nacional Brigantino. In: D. Rodrigo de Sousa Coutinho, *Textos Políticos, Económicos e Financeiros (1783–1811)*. Lisboa: Banco de Portugal, 1993, Vol. II, 110–119 (edited by Andrée Diniz Silva).

Farinha, António Dias, 1992. O primeiro banco em Portugal (1465). In: *Estudos em Homenagem a Jorge Borges de Macedo*. Lisboa: INIC e Faculdade de Letras da Universidade de Lisboa, 153–171.

Fortune, Thomas, 1801. *História Breve e Autêntica do Banco de Inglaterra*. Lisboa: Tipografia do Arco do Cego (translation by Hipólito José da Costa).

Gherity, James A., 1994. The evolution of Adam Smith's theory of banking. *History of Political Economy*, 26:3, 423–441.

Godinho, Vitorino Magalhães, 1955. *Prix et Monnaies au Portugal (1750–1850)*. Paris: Librairie Armand Collin.

Justino, David, 1994. *História da Bolsa de Lisboa*. Lisboa: Bolsa de Valores de Lisboa.

Lisboa, José da Silva, 1810. *Observações sobre a Prosperidade do Estado pelos Liberais Princípios da Nova Legislação do Brasil*. In: José da Silva Lisboa, *Escritos Económicos Escolhidos, 1804–1820*. Lisboa: Banco de Portugal, 1993, Vol. I, 427–472 (edited by António Almodovar).

Macedo, Jorge Borges, 1963. *Elementos para a História Bancária de Portugal, 1797–1820*. Lisboa: Instituto de Alta Cultura.

Madureira, Nuno Luís, 1994. Crédito e mercados financeiros em Lisboa. *Ler História*, nº 26, 21–43.

Marcos, Rui Manuel de Figueiredo, 2008. *Rostos Legislativos de D. João VI no Brasil*. Coimbra: Almedina.

Marcos, Rui Manuel de Figueiredo, 2014. Primeiros passos na História do Direito Bancário Português. *Boletim da Faculdade de Direto da Universidade de Coimbra*, 90:1, 55–69.

Monteiro, Nuno Gonçalo, 1992. O endividamento aristocrático (1750–1832): alguns aspetos. *Análise Social*, nº 116/117, 27:2/3, 263–283.

Murphy, Antoin E., 1997. *John Law: Economic Theorist and Policy-Maker*. Oxford: Clarendon Press.

Neal, Larry, 1990. *The Rise of Financial Capitalism. International Capital Markets in the Age of Reason*. Cambridge and New York: Cambridge University Press.

Neal, Larry, 2021. A collateral story of the rise of Portuguese sovereign debt. *Unpublished Working Paper*.

Neves, José Acúrsio das, 1814–1817. *Variedades sobre objetos relativos às artes, comércio e manufaturas, consideradas segundo os princípios da economia política. In Obras Completas de José Acúrsio das Neves*. Porto: Edições Afrontamento, 1984, Vol. 3 (edited by António Almodovar and Armando Castro).

Pedreira, Jorge Miguel, 1995. *Os Homens de Negócio da Praça de Lisboa, de Pombal ao Vintismo (1755–1822). Diferenciação, Reprodução e Identificação de um Grupo Social*. Lisboa: FCSH/UNL (PhD dissertation).

Pedreira, Jorge Miguel, 1996. Tratos e contratos: atividades, interesses e orientações dos investimentos dos negociantes da praça de Lisboa. *Análise Social*, nº 136–137, 31:2/3, 355–379.

Peres, Damião, 1971. *História do Banco de Portugal (1821–1846)*. Lisboa: Banco de Portugal.

Pinheiro, Magda, 1991. *Os Portugueses e as Finanças no Dealbar do Liberalismo*. Lisboa: Edições João Sá da Costa.

*Plano de ereção de montepios pecuniários para o maior fomento da agricultura, artes e comércio*, 1781. In: *Memórias Económicas Inéditas (1780–1808)*, Lisboa: Academia das Ciências de Lisboa, 1987, 167–182 (edited by José Luís Cardoso).

*Plano para a ereção de um Banco Real em Lisboa*, 1800. Lisboa: Régia Oficina Tipográfica.

Quinn, Stephen and Roberds, William, 2009. An economic explanation of the early bank of Amsterdam, debasement, bills of exchange and the emergence of the first central bank. In: Jeremy Atack and Larry Neal (eds.), *The Origin and Developments of Financial Markets and Institutions. From the Seventeenth Century to the Present*. Cambridge and New York: Cambridge University Press, 32–70.

Reis, D. L. C. Moura, 1836. *Repertório Comercial ou Novo Tratado das moedas efetivas, e conta, pesos e medidas, preço e curso de câmbios das 36 praças da Europa mais comerciantes (. . .)*. Porto: Tipografia Comercial Portuense.

Ribeiro, Joaquim Tibúrcio de Campos, 1787. *Breve mas cabal resposta sobre os juros do dinheiro*. Lisboa: Oficina de Francisco Luís Ameno.

Rocha, Maria Manuela, 1996. Atividade creditícia em Lisboa (1770–1830). *Análise Social*, n° 136–137, 31:2/3, 579–598.

Rocha, Maria Manuela, 1998. Crédito privado em Lisboa numa perspetiva comparada. *Análise Social*, n° 145, 33:1, 91–115.

Roover, Raymond de, 1974. New interpretations of the history of banking. In: *Business, Banking and Economic Thought in Late Medieval and Early Modern Europe*. Chicago and London: University of Chicago Press, 200–238.

Silveira, Luís Espinha, 1987. Aspetos da evolução das finanças públicas portuguesas nas primeiras décadas do século XIX (1800–1827). *Análise Social*, n° 97, 23:3, 505–529.

Smith, Adam, 1776. *An Inquiry Into the Nature and Causes of the Wealth of Nations*. (The Glasgow edition of the Works and Correspondence of Adam Smith). Oxford: Oxford University Press, 1976.

Soares, L. Ribeiro, 1971. *A Moeda em Portugal – breve história*. Lisboa: Banco de Portugal.

Solis, Duarte Gomes, 1622. Discurso sobre lo comercio de las dos Indias (1622). In: Reedição de M. B. Amzalak, *Economia e Finanças, Anais do ISCEF*, 1942, X, 52–54.

Sousa, João Henriques, 1786. *Discurso político sobre o juro do dinheiro*. Lisboa: Régia Oficina Tipográfica.

Vandelli, Domingos, 1796–1797. Alvitrismo económico e financeiro. In: Domingos Vandelli, *Aritmética Política, Economia e Finanças (1770–1804)*. Lisboa: Banco de Portugal, 1994, 273–421 (edited by José Vicente Serrão).

Velde, François R., 2009. Was John Law's system a bubble? The Mississippi bubble revisited. In: Jeremy Atack and Larry Neal (eds.), *The Origin and Development of Financial Markets and Institutions. From the Seventeenth Century to the Present*. Cambridge and New York: Cambridge University Press, 99–120.

Vieira, Pe António, 1646. *Razões apontadas a El-Rei D. João IV a favor dos cristãos-novos, para se lhes haver de perdoar a confiscação de seus bens que entrassem no comércio deste reino*. New edition in: Pe. António Vieira, *Obras Escolhidas*. Lisboa: Clássicos Sá da Costa, 1951, Vol. IV, 63–71.

# 3 The liberal revolution of 1820

## Historical meanings

### 3.1 Economic motivations and background

Portuguese historiography does not record any major divergences or disputes regarding the factors behind the revolution of 1820. The way in which the factors are linked to one another seems to be consensually accepted. Portugal was a European kingdom with its capital in Brazil, a country whose king was absent, which was therefore ruled by a regency that was politically and militarily dominated by Great Britain, the power that had helped the country resist invasion and occupation by Napoleon's forces, whose destructive effects weighed heavily on the Portuguese productive fabric. The aim of the revolution was to bring back the king and put an end to British tutelage, regenerating the country in many aspects according to a new vision of the essence of sovereignty and the ways of exercising power.[1]

The revolution was made to change a state of affairs that had its direct origins in the situation created in late 1807–early 1808, when Prince Regent João and his court left Lisbon and transferred the capital of the imperial kingdom to Rio de Janeiro due to the threat of invasion of the Portuguese territory by Napoleon's troops.

The transfer of the royal family to Brazil was the culmination of a long-lasting Portuguese involvement in a strongly belligerent situation between the main European states, which had polarised around France and Britain. The policy of neutrality and balance that Portugal had attempted to pursue throughout the last decade of the eighteenth century was no longer feasible. Aware of the precariousness of momentary alliances negotiated in exchange for peace, Portugal had realised by the end of 1807 that the time had come to choose sides in the impending, inevitable battle.

The pace with which contradictory diplomatic episodes and engagements took place in late October 1807 clearly demonstrated how hard it was to maintain impossible neutrality. Almost simultaneously, Portugal temporised with France, promising to accept the conditions of the continental blockade imposed by Napoleon and enacting a false declaration of hostility towards Great Britain while secretly arranging with the latter how best to protect the retreat of the royal family to Brazil should this prove to be necessary. In seeking to be on

DOI: 10.4324/9781003355625-3

good terms with the two rival powers, Portugal was actually in a strange situation: it was at war with both countries. Obviously, this exercise in neutrality spelled doom for its territory.

Portugal, as such, was valuable due to the strategic importance of its ports and the richness and potential of its colonial empire, especially Brazil. The small scale of its economic or military power at the European level did not confer upon it any arbitrary prerogatives as a nation. Conversely, its overseas greatness made it even more desirable and, at the same time, more vulnerable to the strategic ambitions and European rivalries that could no longer be avoided. In order to defend the territory, the crown and seat of the imperial homeland had to be transferred to the most important place for its protection, Brazil. Prince Regent João decided accordingly and set sail across the Atlantic on 29 November 1807.

Consideration had already been given to the idea of transferring the court to Brazilian territory at other times, in keeping with a mercantilist imperial belief that the political unity of the Portuguese-Brazilian empire would be strengthened by embracing a principle of specialisation: manufacturing production would be exclusive to the European centre, whereas the extraction of raw materials would take place in the colonies, where the finished products would then be placed. The transfer of the capital to Brazil was a tactical move that would bring clear political advantages. Based on an assessment of the evolution of the international diplomatic situation, it was designed to keep the distant colonies safely protected as an essential guarantee of the empire's continued existence.

Dom Rodrigo de Sousa Coutinho, one of the main architects of the withdrawal that took place at the end of November 1807, had believed this was the way forward 10 years earlier, when he was Minister of the Navy and Overseas Dominions, at a time when he had had to tackle the problems of the administrative and political organisation of the empire. Despite his enlightened vision, suggesting the need for a set of reforms that would make it possible to better manage natural, human and material resources without excessively hindering the Brazilian population, Sousa Coutinho maintained his strong determination to strengthen political unity and consolidate the bonds of economic interdependence between the colonies and the metropolis.

In the abstract order of principles, the transfer of the court was ideal for the pursuit of a relatively enlightened reform programme designed to safeguard and maintain the empire. The fact that the possibility of this transfer had already been aired previously paved the way for accomplishing the project, which finally became a reality in 1807. It was, however, now a very different kind of reality.

Indeed, by the time the court was finally transferred, in what amounted to a very complicated economic and political conjuncture, the assumptions of colonial exclusivity were no longer possible. The transfer took place in a changing world, at a time when there was an ever-growing commitment to the establishment of open economic relations on an international scale. The colonial system that had prevailed until the beginning of 1808 guaranteed the supply of food and raw materials to the metropolis, while simultaneously supplying Brazil with manufactured items that could not be produced locally. It also fed an important sector: the re-export of colonial goods and capital transfers. Above all, it was a crucial source of revenue for the state, through customs duties and the taxes levied on monopoly contracts (Cardoso 2009).

An analysis of the trade balance data at the end of the eighteenth century leaves no doubt about the continuing positive balance that was recorded until 1804, followed by the first signs of a contraction in 1805 and a sharp decline in 1806 and 1807. The surplus in the external trade balance between 1796 and 1804 was accompanied by a positive accumulated trade balance with Brazil (Alexandre 1993 and Pedreira 2000).

The irrefutable proof that the world was indeed changing was given by the promulgation of the Royal Charter of 28 January 1808, the document that formally inaugurated the presence of the Prince Regent in Brazil. On arriving in Bahia, having rested for a mere 7 days after his long Atlantic crossing, the Prince Regent announced that he had news. The document was brief and straight to the point, the reason behind its promulgation being stated as the need to maintain supplies and stimulate economic life. It promised that a global framework would be published shortly afterwards, granting equal treatment for Portuguese vessels as well as for those from friendly nations, reducing import duties from 30 to 24 per cent (except for wine, spirits and olive oil, whose tariffs would double), authorising exports of any products from the Brazilian territory to Portuguese and foreign ports (except for Brazilwood, whose export was banned) and declaring all laws that prevented 'reciprocal trade and navigation in this State of Brazil' to be null and void (*CLP*, Volume V, 477).

The Royal Charter which declared all ports to be open brought a sudden end to the metropolis's exclusive trade status in relation to the colony. Britain and its powerful merchant navy were the great beneficiaries of this measure, as they were now granted direct access to the promising Brazilian market.

In this context, the opening of the ports should not be considered a temporary remedy for the crisis or collapse of the Portuguese trade balance. However, it should instead be seen as a far-reaching solution designed to meet the interests of the economic agents that were already operating in Brazil or those who aspired to position themselves in this important market, mainly British producers and tradesmen. By ending the metropolis's exclusive advantages in trade with its most important colony, the opening of the Brazilian ports to British ships and merchants – euphemistically dubbed in the Royal Charter as 'powers that remain in peace and harmony with my Royal Crown' – consolidated the irreversible shift from an international trade system protected by an exclusive colonial regime to a free trade system with no exclusivity whatsoever.

This measure was less about recovering a lost balance than about building a new economic and political base for the Portuguese-Brazilian Empire, with its capital now situated across the Atlantic. However, these new foundations significantly upset the economic agents and the trade networks that had been developed under the old colonial system.

Analysing the changes in the established institutional order by focusing on the interests at stake does not mean that we should ignore another component that is essential for understanding the transformations taking place at that time: the role of the ideas that had inspired and given doctrinal legitimacy and coherence to the reforms that were being put into practice. In the specific case of the opening of the ports, the economic liberalism favoured and disseminated by political leaders such as José da Silva Lisboa and Dom Rodrigo de Sousa Coutinho played a preponderant role. The political circumstances and the diplomatic context that had dictated the departure of the court from Lisbon justified the opening of the Brazilian economy to foreign markets, as well as the new doctrinal framework of trade relations between Portugal and Great Britain.

The legislation that was published following the opening of the ports continued to show the depth of the changes being made. The charter of 1 April 1808 revoked the previous prohibition of the establishment of manufactures in Brazil and the overseas dominions and authorised 'any of my vassals to establish all kinds of manufactures bar none, doing their work on a small or large scale as they see fit and suits them best' (*CLP*, Volume V, 484). The charter of 28 April 1809 exempted from import duties 'all raw materials that serve as a basis for manufacture of any kind', whose products would also be exempt from export duties. The charter also created incentives for 'the introduction of new expensive and most useful machines' to equip Brazil's emerging industrial structure (*CLP*, Volume V, 733).

The main consequence of this greater openness was a considerable increase in the trade operated by British ships and British merchants and, in general terms, a significant weakening of Portuguese trade with Brazil. In fact, in the period 1808–13, exports and re-exports from Portugal to Brazil declined to 15.9 per cent of the value recorded in 1796–1806 (annual average, at constant prices), while the imports from Brazil and the re-exports of Brazilian products fell to 19.8 per cent and 11.6 per cent, respectively, of the value recorded in 1796–1806 (Pedreira 1994, 325).

This slowdown was further exacerbated by the collapse of the Portuguese industrial structure, due to the devastation caused by the invading French army. Nevertheless, the ultimate reasons for the disaster were to be found in the structural weakness and shortcomings of the Portuguese productive system, which, being inadequately prepared to face the competitiveness of British manufactured products, lacked capital investment and a qualified workforce, had no culture of entrepreneurship and was extremely dependent on state protection and control. Consequently, the opening of the Brazilian ports was a crucial moment that explained the intensification of the process of economic collapse, already apparent in the trade balance data from 1799 onwards.

The transfer of the court to Rio de Janeiro and the settlement in Brazil of roughly 15,000 new inhabitants from Portugal during the first half of 1808 led to a considerable increase in the demand for consumer goods. British merchants and manufacturers did not completely eliminate the possibilities of profitable operations in the Brazilian territory. By way of illustration, it should be noted that, in the opening year of 1808, the number of foreign ships entering the port of Rio de Janeiro was 90; this number rose rapidly to 422 two years later, with the largest share being that of the British ships (Manchester 1933, 76).

The number of British commercial firms and departments in Rio de Janeiro also increased considerably. In August 1808, there were 150 new trading agencies, which corresponded to almost 30 per cent of the total Portuguese and foreign commercial establishments existing in the city (ibid., 76). The British share was even larger if we take into account the number of illegal agents desperately keen to obtain easy riches in the tropics.

Nonetheless, the legislative facilities granted to the establishment of manufactures in Brazil threatened the predominance of British competition, which had initially been ensured by their access to the ports. If there were any doubts, an analysis of the content of the Trade Treaty between Portugal and Great Britain signed in February 1810 would immediately dissipate them. In fact, the treaty brought a clear imbalance to the proclaimed and legislated freedom of production and trade: the clauses of the agreement and the prerogatives that they afforded ensured the British a privileged situation. British manufacturers were granted preferential terms through a reduction in import duties that rendered the competition of Portuguese products unfeasible (*CLP*, Volume V, 827). The tariffs levied on British goods transported by British or Portuguese ships were 15 percent *ad valorem*, while the tariffs on Portuguese or foreign goods transported by Portuguese ships were 16 percent *ad valorem*, and those on other foreign goods carried on foreign ships were 24 percent *ad valorem*.

The development of the country's industrial production structures – namely of the manufacturers that were to be established in Brazil – depended on the conditions imposed by a political alliance that was indispensable to the integrity of Portuguese political sovereignty. The 1810 Treaty, therefore, demonstrates the ambivalence of a path that had to be negotiated under economically adverse conditions before it could be followed.

Dom Rodrigo de Sousa Coutinho played a major part in the process. The influential minister and advisor to Prince João was the main political and economic mentor of the changes introduced in the early years of the court's stay in Brazil. He inspired the publication of the Royal Charter that opened up the ports and the legislation that stimulated manufacturing in Brazil. It was also his hand that, on the Portuguese side, signed the 1810 Treaty that granted trading privileges to British manufactured goods.

The motives for the new economic and social balance arising from the treaty were publicly stated in the Royal Charter of 7 March 1810, written by Sousa Coutinho. The document was of great significance for two fundamental reasons: first, it synthesised and justified the measures and commitments established by the Portuguese court in Rio de Janeiro; second, it sought to minimise the effects of the Portuguese-British treaty by announcing measures that would ensure the economic development of the kingdom, especially in the metropolis. The language of political economy was used in the explanatory narrative of both arguments.

As a justification for the reforms undertaken in Brazil, and due to the court's transfer to Rio de Janeiro, the Royal Charter stated that 'it was necessary to seek to elevate those parts of the empire free from oppression', to which end it was necessary to 'adopt the clearest principles of sound political economy, such as freedom and openness of trade, and the reduction of customs duties, together with the most liberal principles' (*CLP*, Volume V, 859). The aim of liberalising the Brazilian economy was, of course, to increase the supply of agricultural and manufactured goods in order to adjust to the increasing demand. This explains the lifting of the ban on the establishment of factories in Brazil and the promotion of a free production and trade system whose legitimacy was guided by principles of 'sound political economy'. It was in order that the development of the kingdom's manufactures would not be regarded as having been overlooked that the Royal Charter mentioned measures to exempt products manufactured in the metropolis from the payment of import duties in Brazilian ports (Decrees of 28 January 1809 and 7 August 1810 – *CLP*, Volume V, 723 and 900). The measures were welcomed by Brazilian intellectuals, who had been the first to argue in favour of the adoption of the doctrinal principles of *laissez-faire*.

The second explanation for the significance of the Royal Charter drafted by the skilful hand of Sousa Coutinho lies in the fact that this political document was designed to reassure the economic interests of its recipients in the metropolis by indicating a course for the country's development strategy.

'Think not that the introduction of British manufactures may hinder your industry' (*CLP*, Volume V, 859): this seems to be the key message conveyed by the Royal Charter. However, the downgrading also meant the recognition of the failure of a process of development or industrial relaunch that would subsequently exit centre stage. This was clearly stated in the sentence

> [f]or the time being, the use of your money is rightly applied in cultivating your lands, in improving your vineyards, in the well-known manufacture of olive oil, in cultivating artificial meadows, in producing the best wool, in growing mulberry trees and producing silk,

or when an agriculture-centred activity was deemed as

> the only solid one, and the one that puts down strong roots, and that, as it progresses by its due intermediate steps, grows to its full height and then casts those bright rays which blinded the eyes of common people and made even enlightened men believe that manufactures were all there was, and that, in order to have them, the sacrifice of agriculture was useful and convenient.
> (*CLP*, Volume V, 859)

Dom Rodrigo de Sousa Coutinho's unexpected agrarian confession was intended to show that the prosperity of manufacturers depended on the competitiveness of their products, which in turn depended on the development of agriculture, providing food at low prices and low wages, a permanent flow of raw materials and a strong internal market. He could not ignore the immediate effects of the 1810 Treaty and bluntly admitted that 'the reduction of customs duties will lead to a large influx of foreign manufactures'. However, should any Portuguese manufacturer close down or grind to a halt as a consequence, it would be 'proof that this manufacture had no solid foundation, nor was it of any real advantage to the State' (*CLP*, Volume V, 860).

Hence, all the arguments in the Royal Charter of 7 March 1810 show a clear preference for a model of development centred on agriculture. The golden rule of the liberalisation of the external market – conceived according to the principles of 'sound political economy' but established under undisguised British pressure – implied the precarious competitiveness of Portuguese manufactured goods. Industrialisation was viewed to be less important than agricultural development, which would ensure both an advantageous productive specialisation and a possible future development of manufactures.

The strategic gamble had far-reaching consequences for the much-needed agricultural reforms, leading to the removal of institutional and fiscal obstacles and mainly to the reform of the charter regime. Dom Rodrigo anticipated the discussion of one of the crucial issues involved in the dismantling of the *ancien regime* economy, which would only be realised in the new political environment emanating from the revolution of 1820. This new environment also allowed for a critical appraisal of the disruptive consequences of the choices relating to political and economic development that resulted from the opening of the ports and the friendship and trade treaties of 1810. Once again, these choices reflected the inevitability of circumstances and political commitments on a global scale beyond Portugal's control.

## 3.2 On the eve of the revolution

The political *détente* in Europe following the end of the Napoleonic wars enabled Portugal to distance itself to some extent from its traditional alliance with Great Britain, which had been instrumental in preserving Portuguese sovereignty in the troubled context of the French invasions. However, this new context did not impede Portugal's somewhat bland participation in the talks held at the Congress of Vienna between May 1814 and June 1815 (Alexandre 1993).

Portugal was forced to comply with the British pressure for the abolition of the slave trade, although this measure was geographically limited to trade conducted north of the equator. The compensation for seized vessels was manifestly insufficient to cover the losses incurred in terms of both the capital invested and the expected profits. The surrender of French Guyana, the non-devolution of the colony of Sacramento, the postponement of the incorporation of Olivenza into the kingdom of Portugal and the breakdown in the negotiations to repeal the 1810 treaties of friendship and trade all demonstrate how frustrating the aftermath of the Congress of Vienna negotiations had been from the point of view of satisfying Portuguese interests.

Portugal was still prey to the inevitable uncertainties resulting from contradictory affinities. In the struggles between the supporters of diplomatic alignments that would be decisive for defining Portugal's fate as a multi-territorial imperial nation, those who championed the pro-French option now argued that the court should stay in Brazil, thus restraining pro-independence tensions and preventing the British from gaining complete control over trade. Conversely, the proponents of pro-British alignments supported the return of the court to Lisbon, thereby reinforcing a strategic alliance that would counter new Franco-Spanish incursions while leaving Brazil at the mercy of those who, in actual practice, exerted control over the principal economic activities.

News of the preparations being made for the return of King João VI's court to Lisbon at the end of 1814 – thus yielding to pressure from the British, who, after the withdrawal, would certainly be more comfortable about pursuing their commercial and political interests in Brazil – was more than a mere rumour. However, Portugal's ability to withstand this pressure had also brought greater difficulties in managing its political and economic relationship with the European powers, especially for the regency in Lisbon, which was responsible for safeguarding the country's sovereignty, already in danger of being eroded.

The creation of the United Kingdom of Portugal, Brazil and the Algarves in December 1815 sanctioned the option of staying in Rio de Janeiro. This was the formal recognition of the end of a colonial status that had been substantially modified with the court's residence in Rio since the beginning of 1808, the opening of the Brazilian ports to the British merchant navy and the signing of the friendship and trade treaties with Great Britain in 1810.

The ending of the colonial status dictated by the creation of the United Kingdom of Portugal, Brazil and the Algarves was not intended to suggest that this was also the end of an empire. Nonetheless, the attempts to reinvent and revitalise this same empire exposed the imminent risk of it entering its final stage. The unification of Portugal and Brazil in a single imperial kingdom contributed to the illusion of a cohesive political unit governed under the auspices of a protective monarch, together with the symbol of a new Royal Coat of Arms representing both the Portuguese and the Brazilian arms. The project was doomed from the start, a utopia that did not point to the future, but rather to the revival of the idea of an empire that was no longer meant to be.

The United Kingdom of Portugal, Brazil and the Algarve was a solution that met the requirements for the assisted maintenance of a waning Luso-Brazilian empire. It was also a skilful way for Portugal to preserve some balance in its relations with the European powers, guaranteeing its already dwindling control over the riches of an immense Brazil. It may also have contributed to the suppression of some of the more inflammatory demands for independence, which were heavily influenced by events in Spanish America at the time.

In any case, for all of these reasons, the United Kingdom of Portugal, Brazil and the Algarves had only a fleeting existence and eventually became law with no object of the application.

The best proof of this failure may well be the expressions of discontent and anger that questioned the ability of the court and the regency to secure political equilibrium in a territorially divided kingdom. Protests were heard both on the streets of the capital of the United Kingdom and in the atmosphere of exile in London, which many Brazilian-born intellectuals had grown accustomed to, writing and reflecting in influential newspapers (*Correio Braziliense*, *Português* and *O Investigador Português em Inglaterra*), and thus expressing the enlightened opinions of those who were dissatisfied with the current political and economic situation at the time. The periodical press had been established with the support of the Portuguese merchants established in London, who were interested in raising public awareness about the harmful consequences of the new economic process unleashed both by the 1808 decree that had opened up the Brazilian ports and by the treaties of 1810.

The defence of the kingdom and the maintenance of its status as an independent nation required a huge military effort that was largely supported by the British government. In fact, in the years following the expulsion of Napoleon's troops from Portuguese territory (1812 and 1813), the stipend guaranteed by the British authorities for the payment of troops, clothing, footwear, food, weapons and ammunition came very close to the total military expenditure of the Royal Exchequer (Costa 2008, 17).

This aid meant that the Portuguese army was commanded by a British officer, William Carr Beresford, and that the ambassadors of the British monarch either had a formal membership (Charles Stuart, from 1810 to 1814) or were officially consulted (George Canning) by the regency government. The reason behind this was, of course, the need to control the military spending financed by the allied powers and the strategic options that might affect their compliance with the provisions of the friendship and trade treaties of 1810.

The regency's inability to make decisions on key issues was an inherent feature of its limited power in political, financial, military and legal spheres, which depended not only on the guidelines of the Prince Regent and the government in Rio de Janeiro, but also on the consultations held with British diplomatic and political agents.

Therefore, there was an ever-greater feeling of orphanhood and humiliation on the part of the regency, as its inability to meet and decide became more visible with each passing day. Appointments were made, but positions were not filled; successive requests were made for resignation, revealing disinterest and indifference on the part of those in positions of authority; and illnesses were frequently cited as a reason for inaction. All of these reactions added a sense of frailty and incapacity to the regency's already limited power. Such vulnerability led a few magistrates who were not affiliated to the regency to compile a series of scattered, disorderly and extravagant laws in order to mitigate the iniquity and arbitrariness of their application.

This was reason enough for some corporate interests to express their dissatisfaction with the difficulties that they experienced in the organisation, functioning and governance of the economic sphere, with the military structure and, indirectly, with the political and judicial administration of the kingdom.

In Brazil, discontent reached significant proportions: there were uprisings in Pernambuco in March 1817, protesting against the rising cost of living, starvation and the overwhelming centrality that the Rio court had brought to the normally disperse Brazilian economy. On the other side of the kingdom, separated from Brazil by the vast Atlantic Ocean, the former imperial capital stagnated under a regency that was subject to the strategic interests of the British, duly protected by the friendship and trade treaties, which imposed prerogatives and privileges that hindered the operations of Portuguese tradesmen and industrialists.

In the metropolis, the prestigious General Gomes Freire de Andrade sought to unite people in their feelings of popular dissatisfaction. He lacked the capacity and ambition for political leadership, although he attracted support from various quarters, in particular from the Freemasons (who were still only taking their first steps at the time), of which he had been the Grand Master since 1816. Gomes Freire also enjoyed the active support of a small group of supposed rebels who had served in Napoleon's army in the theatres of war in Prussia, Austria and Russia. Even so, he was still far from mobilising any significant military and civilian support, thus limiting the political and revolutionary scope of his proposed movement.

After this conspiratorial movement was discovered, those involved were subjected to extreme violence, arguably intended to strike fear into anyone who might wish to replicate the feat. Despite the failure of the rebellion, great compassion was shown for the terrible treatment inflicted on the supposed conspirators, who were summarily sentenced without a trial and executed in a public square in Lisbon. It was also clear that the threat of premeditated political change could not be ignored, representing a serious challenge to the vulnerabilities and difficulties experienced by the governors of the kingdom responsible for conducting political activities.

The reports of the meetings of the Regency Council reveal tensions that resulted in extremely tenuous agreements being made between the members themselves, the government in Rio de Janeiro and the British military leaders, namely Wellington and Beresford (Nogueira 1810–1820). Besides expressing his feelings about his interlocutors, Raimundo Nogueira gave an account of the matters under discussion, highlighting the most relevant political issues, namely the plans being drawn up for loan applications, public debt creation, the issue of paper money, the regularisation of tax debts, the launch of new taxes and the constraints on public spending. He described an atmosphere in which the financial system was subject to constant pressure from military expenditure, supply shortages and the payment of wages. Most of the revenue came from the stipend paid by the British government, which explains the constant requests for clarification and protests made by the British military chiefs regarding failures observed in the administration of the Royal Exchequer. For those who were responsible for paying such heavy expenses, it was only natural that they should remain forever vigilant.

Raimundo Nogueira expressed his opposition to the doctrinal principles of certain economic liberalism that, as already mentioned, had led to the signing of the 1810 treaties of friendship and trade. He sought to ensure that they would not be used as a pretext for strengthening the British claim to further exemptions from the payment of duties or their demands for the lowering of fixed tariffs (Nogueira 1810–1820, 218–19). His discomfort, resulting from the pressure that the regency was constantly subjected to, is clearly evident in his account of the meeting of 28 September 1817, in which he elaborated on the promises of added power that Beresford had been given by the Prince Regent:

> It was discussed what the Government should do in the light of His Majesty's orders brought by Marshal Beresford, through which the latter was given great powers independent from the government in all military branches, including a major part of the jurisdiction of civil magistrates, which is thereby greatly restricted, depresses the authority of the regency that represents His Majesty in Portugal, exhausts the Exchequer, ruins the people, establishes a military government and alienates the love of the people towards their sovereign, not only because of the evils such innovations bring about, stopping the sources of wealth of the Nation and rendering it impossible for the Exchequer to support credit, but also because of the aversion with which they see a foreigner being given powers so extraordinary and never before granted to other Generals-in-Chief of much higher rank, who commanded our armies on many occasions.
>
> (Nogueira 1810–1820, 281)

Through one of its most enlightened members, the regency anticipated and voiced, in the silence of its office, the reasons for the discontent that are usually listed in order to justify the conspiracy movement of 1817. In fact, the appeal contained in the proclamations of the rebels who banded together to form the Regeneration Council mentions the exhaustion of the Exchequer, the excessive requisition of hands for military service, the weight of the contributions to guarantee the defence of the territory and the annihilation of agriculture, trade and industry.

As there was no love lost between Ricardo Raimundo Nogueira and Gomes Freire de Andrade, it is interesting to note the similarity of the reasons that led the member of the regency council to state as follows at the last meeting in which he participated, on 5 February 1820:

> I remain on board the ship and share the fate of my fellow passengers who sail this stormy sea; but I am no longer the pilot, nor do I answer to God, the King or the Nation regarding the success of the voyage.
>
> (Nogueira 1810–1820, 96)

The voyage would come to an end a few months later. The king was still absent. The British controlled the regency and the army. The administration of public life and justice was entangled in an obsolete legal framework. Brazilian colonial trade had lost its vital attributes. Magistrates, military figures and businessmen joined forces in calling for a change that seemed inevitable and would have to be regenerative.

It should be noted that, although the scant data available does not make it possible to accurately reconstruct the evolution of agricultural and industrial production in the period between the end of the French invasions and the revolution of 1820, there is no documentary evidence to support the picture of an economically and financially ruined country that was painted by the protagonists and enthusiasts of the regeneration movement. The pessimistic, negative discourse on the state of the country was designed to create a space for debate on the need for institutional and political change. The reconstruction of the evolution of GDP in the same period leads to the conclusion that an average annual growth rate of 3 per cent was recorded between 1813 and 1822, which means that the economy had begun to show signs of a significant recovery shortly after the sharp decline during the period of French occupation (Graph 3.1).

The well-informed political economist José Acúrsio das Neves was right. As he witnessed how hard it was for the people in the country and in the city to eke out a living, he believed that future prosperity was inevitable:

> However, let us not be discouraged, for with the aid of a good administrative system, misfortunes can be mended faster than one might think.

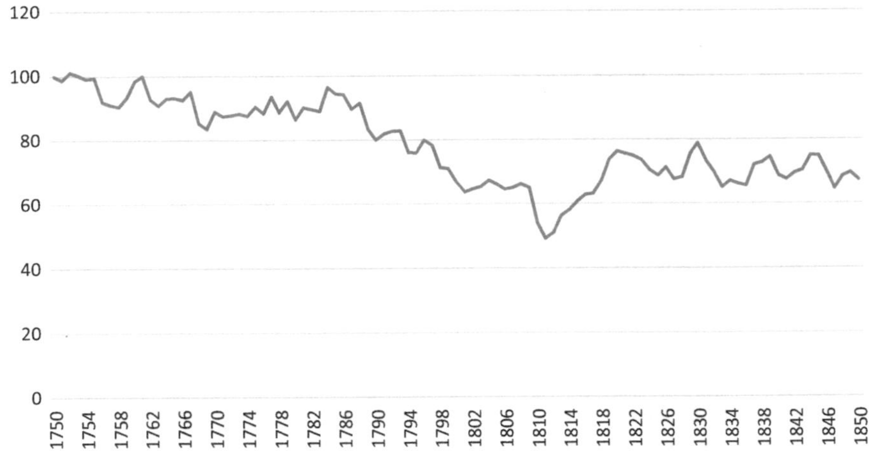


*Graph 3.1.* Evolution of GDP per capita, Portugal 1750–1850

Source: Palma and Reis 2019. Index 1750.

> Nature has condemned all states and kingdoms, nay, all human things, to perpetually falter in alternating successions of prosperity and adversity; change is often unexpected and imperceptible.
>
> (Neves 1814–1817, 346)

This was a different way of portraying the rhetorical argument of the kingdom's economic ruin: to express the hope that the depressive phase of the cycle of adversity might gradually fade away and that a new administrative system would guarantee a return to prosperity. Acúrsio das Neves did not believe that a revolution would solve the problem. Yet, it was a revolution that ended up triumphing and contributing to overcoming the kingdom's difficulties in staying united and prosperous.

## 3.3 The Portuguese case in an international context

In a book dedicated to the day of 24 August 1820, which he dubbed 'eternally sacred and memorable', the young writer and politician Almeida Garrett wrote in a tone of patriotic exaltation:

> We now have a homeland, of which despotism had robbed us; timidity, cowardice, ignorance, which had created it, which was prostrated with vile idolatry before its work, is over. The last hour of tyranny has sounded; the fanaticism that was spread across the face of the earth has disappeared; the sun of liberty shone on our horizon, and the very last darkness of despotism was dispelled by its rays and now lies in hell.
>
> (Garrett 1821, 4)

Was it really a revolution? Does the adjective 'liberal' best describe the meaning of that moment? The approach adopted in this book implies a positive answer to both questions while accepting the validity of a designation that expresses the scope and meaning of the changes that began at the time.[2]

The revolution lacked the usual meanings assigned to the word: insurrection, uprising, social revolt, political rebellion, violent tumult or civil war. It was a simple, quiet uprising of dissatisfied troops, who had been convinced by magistrates and businessmen from Porto of the inevitability and relevance of this heroic gesture. It was a military revolt that peacefully dictated the beginning of the end of a period in history. Also, according to Garrett, in the same book that was intended to explain the legitimacy of the revolutionary movement initiated on 24 August:

> The nation behaved with prudence, generosity and peace, which are the soul and the pledge of public happiness, and which are the hallmark of a good revolution.
>
> (Garrett 1821, 26)

As in any 'good revolution', the events of 1820 and the period of gestation and approval of the first Portuguese Constitution of 1822 provoked reactions and divisions that resulted in setbacks and retreats. There were coups and riots, finally leading to a civil war (1832–34) that was the violent, bloody outcome of the revolution initiated in 1820. It was in the period between 1820 and 1834 that the Portuguese Liberal Revolution affirmed and consolidated its purpose and its fate.

Garrett called it a 'good' revolution. One of the main inspirers of the uprising of 24 August 1820, Manuel Fernandes Tomás, would later refer to this event as a 'fortunate' revolution (Tomás 1821, 8). One of the most important newspapers created at the time, *Astro da Lusitânia,* called it a 'miraculous' revolution (n° 1, 30 October 1820). Yet, the word 'revolution' was scarcely used by the protagonists of the moment. They nearly always preferred the word 'regeneration', with which they sought to convey the meaning of a movement that gives new life to a social and political body in need of special care. The term 'revolution' and the adjective 'revolutionary' tended to be used pejoratively by those seeking to draw a parallel between the Portuguese regenerators and the French revolutionaries, whose example had to be exorcised.

Those seeking to interpret what happened in Portugal immediately before and after 24 August 1820 have used the concept of revolution in its multiple and multifaceted sense of a military uprising, institutional reform, political restoration and economic and social regeneration, thus acknowledging the broad scope of long-term changes with implications for the functioning of everyday institutions and structures. This means that the word 'revolution' includes movement and change, a sense of regeneration and progress, and is not necessarily associated with the limited idea of violent turmoil or civil war.

This regenerative dimension was a crucial part of the revolution of 1820: the search for adaptation and change, the enjoyment of freedom, the eagerness to create new representative institutions of power and the consolidation of civic virtues. It involved state participation and, in a way, it was confused or mixed with the idea of reform that the State must fulfil, that is, it presupposed the legislator's authority and political responsibility in designing and implementing programmes of social improvement for the benefit of the population as a whole. It also had a feature that is a core attribute of any revolution: the script for the future accomplishment of present-day promises and undertakings, the explicit desire of its main mentors and promoters to continue to change the order of things (Baker and Edelstein 2015).

Why was the revolution 'liberal'? This adjective suggests a model of society that is based on each individual's strengths and capacities, enhancing those virtues that can generate social welfare, and limiting state intervention whenever individual freedom is at stake. The direct protagonists of the Portuguese Revolution of 1820 did not feel the need to state the reasons why they proclaimed themselves to be liberals or described the principles and ideas that they held as liberal. The influence of the Spanish language and of that nation's experiences, in which the word 'liberal' had been widely used to characterise the constitutional principles approved by the Cadiz Parliament in 1812 and the resistance and liberation movement before the French occupation, certainly helped. The word 'liberal' is sometimes associated with the defence of a new concept of sovereignty based on a nation made up of individuals and the denunciation of arbitrariness and despotism. It is used to describe a model of political organisation based on the separation of powers (legislative, executive and judicial) and the defence of individual rights and guarantees. Political change is used to proclaim freedom of expression in the public sphere as a major liberal cause. Finally, albeit less so than in the past, all principles that are linked to the notion of the economic activities of production and consumption not being subject to state control and supervision are deemed as liberal.

The military uprising of 24 August 1820 had the undeniable status of a liberal revolution. Yet, at the end of the day, what happened in Portugal 200 years ago was part of a wider transformation and revolutionary movement that spread across the world, mainly in Europe, but also in North and South America and several regions in Asia (from the Ottoman Empire to Russia, and from India to China, Japan and Indonesia). These changes took place on a global scale: their influence was to be felt in different ways and cannot be circumscribed to the places that are usually mentioned by the canonical European-based historiography. The idea that liberal revolutions (in Europe or elsewhere) had a single causal origin, simplified by the symbols and slogans of the French Revolution that the Napoleonic expansion and subsequent geopolitical ambitions helped to disseminate and implement, no longer passes muster.

One of the defining features of this era of revolutions on a global scale was the belief in the virtues of a new notion of sovereignty whose philosophical foundations were based on the natural rights of individuals to choose their legitimate representatives. The anti-monarchical, anti-clerical and anti-aristocratic struggle against the social and political order of the *ancien régime* was especially relevant to the protagonists of the French Revolution of 1789. In an environment conducive to denouncing the arbitrariness of absolute power, they sought to establish new political principles of citizenship and new universal rights, considering it essential to publish written constitutions that would establish enduring processes for the separation and distribution of powers.

Many of the ideas arising from the French Revolution had repercussions in other regions and institutions in Europe and elsewhere. Nonetheless, they also aroused animosity and opposition in countries where it was believed that political reforms could be made without the exaggerations of Jacobin terror and the harmful effects of Bonaparte's hegemonic expansion. In some cases, namely in Spain, Portugal and Italy, there was even an absolute contradiction, as the political and ideological teachings of the French Revolution were evoked so that nations would be patriotically spared the devastation caused by the Napoleonic occupation and its aftermath.

Another defining element of the era of revolutions was the dismantling of empires and the consequent independence of vast colonial territories. The

American Revolution of 1776 showed how a small-scale revolt against the fiscal system in force in one part of the empire could grow to become a global movement directed against local powers and, by extension, the British Crown. The extent of trade relations within existing empires and the crises caused by independence movements and their demands for self-determination led to the realisation that the world had become a place where convergent revolutions brought irreversible changes, no matter how hard the former empires strove to keep these movements at bay.

The perception that things could actually change stimulated the awakening of nations, the formation of national identities and the growing assertion of countries that wished for their capacities to be recognised internationally. However, these patriotic appeals and designs were disseminated by disgruntled voices that echoed and promoted the emulation of good practices, in other words of revolutionary events that had succeeded elsewhere. Inferiority complexes and backward-thinking sentiments were also rhetorical instruments used to raise awareness and involve the public in introducing changes and achieving regenerative aims. Nationalism and cosmopolitanism coexisted in a seemingly paradoxical way and complemented one another as the foundations for the construction of a different, global world.

A different kind of revolution – one which had no fixed calendar – was also taking place in those days: the substantial increase in productivity and prosperity associated with the so-called Industrial Revolution, whose effects were clearly evident in the last quarter of the eighteenth century. The ever-greater application of capital and technology in the industrial sector, the innovations in motive power brought about by the steam engine and the rapid spread of its use – as well as the benefits of new forms of organisation and the division of labour – led to significant increases in the supply of manufactured products. It was now possible to respond to the growing demands driven by new consumer habits and even to encourage an upsurge in superfluous consumption, with the subsequent, inevitable expansion of markets and trade.

The analytical categories used by the science of political economy to explain the functioning of the markets were part of a doctrinal framework that declared the virtues of the natural order of the market according to principles that became known as economic liberalism. These principles were based on the notion of freedom in both production and trade, without any obstacles or constraints being imposed by state regulations or corporate privileges. This ideology would be instrumental in ensuring the advancement of liberal revolutions on a global scale, even though in many situations the self-confessed supporters of *laissez-faire* and economic freedom in trade preferred to maintain a frame of reference that was unreceptive to liberal ideas in the political field.

The way in which these transformations were assimilated varied from country to country, and from region to region. The delays or different paces in the introduction of change depended on a variety of factors, namely boldness in questioning the political order of the old regime and the structures of the absolutist State; the ability to denounce local privileges or specific jurisdictions; the capacity to mobilise military forces committed to supporting or triggering a change in regime; the existence of a cultural, intellectual or religious environment conducive to the reception of enlightened ideas about regeneration and social improvement; and the economic successes resulting from an industrial revolution that generated increased levels of production and consumption. In fact, all these factors need to be considered as a whole if an appropriate interpretation is to be made of the complexity of a historical period to which the Portuguese liberal revolution of 1820 also contributed.

In order to understand the reasons behind every revolution, we should take into account the way in which popular pressures and dissatisfactions were seen and managed, the impact of manifestos, complaints and petitions, the way in which kings and princes were seen as the trustees of solutions for good government, and their maturity in defence of the essential goodness of universal constitutional principles. Above all, we should consider the ways in which these various elements frequently came together in specific contexts that might lead to rupture. In other words, the analysis of the most striking events of the Portuguese liberal revolution benefits from our overall knowledge of the context of contemporary revolutionary movements in Southern Europe.

In Spain, the war of liberation fought against France had destructive effects in many different areas, from family life to military organisation. The Cadiz Constitution was approved in March 1812, at the height of the Napoleonic occupation of Spain under the rule of the imposed king Joseph Bonaparte, the emperor's brother. Cadiz was still a hotbed of resistance and a symbol of the hard-fought war of independence waged by the Spanish liberal revolutionaries, supported by English military aid. Unbeknown to the occupying power, Cadiz hosted a session of the *Cortes* in 1812, at which a constitutional text was approved that would influence political developments in several southern European countries.

The constitution was of a markedly liberal nature, being based on the principle of separation of powers – with the greatest emphasis being given to the legislative power – and on a concept of sovereignty that conferred upon the nation – i.e. the people – the role of the trustee of this essential power. Despite its republican and anti-aristocratic inclinations (possibly due to the influence and inspiration of the French Constitution of 1791), the document recognised Ferdinand VII as king. Ferdinand VII rejected the constitutional precepts 2 years later when he was enthroned at the end of the Napoleonic occupation.

King Ferdinand VII pursued a policy of imperial reinforcement that was no longer able to promote Spain in international markets. In Spain's American colonies, the pro-independence sentiments and the pressure that they exerted could no longer be held in check. The declarations of independence in Haiti (1804), Colombia (1810), Venezuela (1811), Paraguay (1811), Mexico (1813), Argentina (1816) and Chile (1818) clearly illustrate the new geopolitical environment of a disintegrating empire on the eve of 1820.

Internally, the discontent that many social and political sectors felt in relation to King Ferdinand VII's obstinacy was expressed in an uprising in January 1820: led by Rafael Riego, mutinous troops refused to embark on new colonial expeditions and gave their military backing to the movement that established the Cadiz Constitution as a guide to liberal political reforms two months later, in March 1820. The constitution lasted just over 3 years, which demonstrates how difficult it was to renovate the Spanish political regime and highlights the strong internal tensions that existed between 'moderates' and 'progressives', who remained unable to achieve any form of reconciliation and convergent understanding.

Spanish radicalism was not a major cause for concern among the main European powers (England, France, Russia and Austria), which merely awaited the predictable anti-liberal outcome. Nonetheless, the proclamation of the Cadiz Constitution arguably breathed new life into liberal political ideas in several European countries and became a core reference for the liberal, patriotic and nationalist movements that appeared at this time, especially in Southern Europe. This was the case in Naples and Sicily (July 1820), as well as in Lombardy and Piedmont (1821), where the Spanish example was viewed as a strategic political reference. The discontent that spread across several Italian republics and sovereignties did not spring merely from a premeditated revolutionary conspiratorial spirit or an adherence to the principles of political liberalism that had been embraced elsewhere in Europe. It largely arose from the influence of the Spanish experience of international communication among secret societies and from the ineffectiveness of the Austrian tutelage that had been established in many regions of Italy in the aftermath of the Congress of Vienna. This had eventually given rise to natural feelings of displeasure that were waiting for the right time to make themselves heard.

Similar uprisings occurred in Greece (February 1821) and in other territories of the Ottoman empire, with the active participation of secret societies and international networks that would eventually be at the origin of movements demanding national independence from Turkish rule.

The efforts of Metternich, the leading figure in the Austrian Empire, to prevent the growth of liberal movements in Southern Europe eventually succeeded, aided by the diplomatic understanding of the other European powers that formed part of the Holy Alliance and preferred changes introduced through a process of a smooth transition to political upheavals that might disturb the prevailing orders in Europe in the wake of the Congress of Vienna.

It was in this Southern European environment, where an atmosphere had been developed that encouraged the sharing of liberal yearnings for political change and the transformation of the modes of representation and legitimation of power under the watchful eye of the powers of the Holy Alliance, that the conditions and the factors were created that lay at the origin of Portugal's liberal revolution in 1820.

## Notes

1 For a brief presentation of the antecedents and the development of the Portuguese liberal revolution, see Cardoso 2019 and Cordeiro 2020.
2 The historiography of liberal revolutions is immensely rich and diversified. It is not my purpose to discuss or dispute here the conventional wisdom on the subject. Among the many essential references, we can always benefit from revisiting Armitage and Subrahmanyam 2010, Bayly 2004, Fernández Sebastián 2009 and 2014, Hobsbawm 1962, Isabela 2009, Koselleck 1985, Osterhammel 2014 and Paquette 2013.

## References


Alexandre, Valentim, 1993. *Os Sentidos do Império. Questão Nacional e Questão Colonial na Crise do Antigo Regime Português*. Porto: Edições Afrontamento.

Armitage, David and Subrahmanyam, Sanjay (eds.), 2010. *The Age of Revolutions in Global Context, c. 1760–1840*. Basingstoke and New York: Palgrave Macmillan.

Baker, Keith Michael and Edelstein, Dan (eds.), 2015. *Scripting Revolution. A Historical Approach to the Comparative Study of Revolutions*. Stanford: Stanford University Press.

Bayly, C. A., 2004. *The Birth of the Modern World, 1790–1914. Global Connections and Comparisons*. Oxford: Blackwell.

Cardoso, José Luís, 2009. Free trade, political economy and the birth of a new economic nation: Brazil, 1808–1810. *Revista de Historia Económica – Journal of Iberian and Latin American Economic History*, nº 2, 183–204.

Cardoso, José Luís, 2019. *A Revolução Liberal de 1820/The Liberal Revolution of 1820*. Lisboa: CTT.

[*CLP*] *Coleção da Legislação Portuguesa desde a última compilação das Ordenações* (org. António Delgado da Silva). Lisboa: Tipografia Maigrense, 1825.

Cordeiro, José Manuel Lopes, 2020. *1820. Revolução Liberal do Porto*. Porto: Câmara Municipal do Porto.

Costa, Fernando Dores, 2008. Army size, military recruitment and financing in Portugal during the period of the Peninsula War, 1808–1811. *e-journal of Portuguese History*, 6:2.

Fernández Sebastián, Javier (dir.), 2009. *Diccionario Político y Social del Mundo Iberoamericano. La Era de las Revoluciones, 1750–1850 [Iberconceptos I]*. Madrid: Fundación Carolina/Centro de Estudios Políticos y Constitucionales.

Fernández Sebastián, Javier (dir.), 2014. *Diccionario Político y Social del Mundo Iberoamericano. Conceptos Políticos Fundamentales, 1770–1870 [Iberconceptos II]*. Madrid: Centro de Estudios Políticos y Constitucionales.

Garrett, J. de Almeida, 1821. O dia vinte e quatro de Agosto. In: *Obras Completas de Almeida Garrett*. Lisboa: Empresa da História de Portugal, 1904, Vol. XXIV, 1–29.

Hobsbawm, Eric J., 1962. *The Age of Revolution (1789–1848)*. London: Weidenfeld & Nicolson.

Isabela, Maurizio, 2009. *Risorgimento in Exile: Italian Émigrés and the Liberal International in the Post-Napoleonic Era*. Oxford: Oxford University Press.

Koselleck, Reinhart, 1985. Historical criteria of the modern concept of revolution. In: Kozelleck, Reinhart, *Futures Past: On the Semantics of Historical Time*. Cambridge, MA: MIT Press, 39–54.

Manchester, Alan K., 1933. *British Preeminence in Brazil, its Rise and Decline. A Study in European Expansion*. Chapel Hill: The University of North Carolina Press.

Neves, José Acúrsio das, 1814–1817. *Variedades sobre objetos relativos às artes, comércio e manufaturas, consideradas segundo os princípios da economia política*. In *Obras Completas de José Acúrsio das Neves*. Porto: Edições Afrontamento, 1984, Vol. 3 (edited by António Almodovar and Armando Castro).

Nogueira, Ricardo Raimundo, 1810–1820. *Memória das coisas mais notáveis que se trataram nas conferências do governo*. Coimbra: Imprensa da Universidade de Coimbra, 2012 (edited by Ana Cristina Araújo).

Osterhammel, Jürgen, 2014. *The Transformation of the World. A Global History of the Nineteenth Century*. Princeton and Oxford: Princeton University Press.

Palma, Nuno and Reis, Jaime, 2019. From convergence to divergence: Portuguese economic growth, 1527–1850. *Journal of Economic History*, 79:2, 477–506.

Paquette, Gabriel, 2013. *Imperial Portugal in the Age of Atlantic Revolutions. The Luso-Brazilian World, c. 1770–1850*. Cambridge and New York: Cambridge University Press.

Pedreira, Jorge M., 1994. *Estrutura Industrial e Mercado Colonial. Portugal e Brasil 1780–1830*. Lisboa: Difel.

Pedreira, Jorge M., 2000. From growth to collapse: Portugal, Brazil, and the breakdown of the old colonial system (1760–1830). *Hispanic American Historical Review*, 80:4, 839–864.

Tomás, Manuel Fernandes, 1821. *Relatório sobre o Estado e Administração do Reino durante o Tempo da Junta Provisional do Supremo Governo*. Lisboa: Impressão Régia.

# 4 The political context of 1820 and the urgent need to create a bank

## 4.1 Paper money and public debt: debates in the public sphere

As discussed in the previous chapter, the Portuguese liberal revolution of 1820 was possible thanks to the combination of a variety of short-term conditions and structural factors. Among these, emphasis should be given to the dissatisfaction that several social sectors felt towards the political fragility of the kingdom and its colonial dominions and what they considered to be the continuation of obstacles that impeded the full development of national capacities. Portugal was at that time a European country with the seat of its imperial power established in Brazil, in the hands of a regency controlled both politically and militarily by its British ally, who had played such a prominent role in the liberation of Portugal after the French invasions between 1807 and 1811.

The military uprisings of 1820 – in August in Porto and in September in Lisbon – took place in a peaceful and orderly manner. The demands of the insurgents consisted of two fundamental points: the return of the king from Rio de Janeiro to Lisbon, and the establishment of a provisional government that would prepare the meeting of a parliamentary assembly whose main task would be to draw up a constitution.

The establishment of a constitutional monarchy and a new form for the exercise of sovereignty (based on the legislative power) created the appropriate institutional and political conditions for dismantling the *ancien régime*'s economic and social structure, thus strengthening the conviction that it was possible to erect a new model of economic, social and political development.

Although its fundamental purpose was the elaboration of a constitutional code, the first Portuguese parliament discussed and legislated on a wide range of matters relating to social life, seeking to give the form of law to everything that lacked regulation, as well as to respond to the various requests emanating from an effervescent civil society eager to find solutions to its individual and collective problems.

Freedom of expression and freedom of the press were among the first concerns to merit the attention of liberal politicians, who did not hesitate in establishing the conditions for the formation of an active public sphere committed

DOI: 10.4324/9781003355625-4

to the exercise of free and responsible citizenship. The proliferation of newspapers and pamphlets dedicated to a wide range of topics considered to be of public interest, as well as the abundant flow of petitions, manifestos and proposals to the deputies and to the parliamentary committees, were eloquent signs of the strength of a public opinion that claimed the right to play an important part in building a new society.

It is therefore not surprising that, among the issues that caught the attention of anonymous citizens or competent public officials and intellectuals, we find matters relating to the economic and financial situation of the country and the specific problems of public credit, as well as to the necessary remedies for redeeming public debt and for stabilising the credibility of institutions that had been designed for that purpose.

In the months following the revolutionary movements of 1820, strong public pressure was exerted, demanding that a solution be found to the problems that had long afflicted both the holders of increasingly depreciated paper money and the public and private institutions forced to accept payments in the form of paper. In some cases, solutions were presented for the consolidation of the public debt and for the gradual extinction of inconvertible paper money over time, which required the occurrence of one of the following conditions: the existence of an institution already prepared for this mission, such as the Royal Exchequer or the Board of Interest (of Royal Loans), or the creation of a new institution specifically designed for that purpose. It was in this last context that the urgency of setting up a bank was discussed.

It should be remembered that both the Provisional Government and the *Cortes Constituintes* had each expressed their concern about the problem. On 27 October 1820, Manuel Fernandes Tomás, the Minister for the Affairs of the Realm and the Treasury at that time, appointed a commission entrusted with the task of calculating the amount of paper money in circulation, seeking to bring an end to speculation about the value that would need to be redeemed. In turn, the Sovereign Congress also sought to restore public credit and reduce the level of the State's non-fulfilment of its obligations to its private creditors. On 5 May 1821, it approved the upgrading of the crown's property to the category of national property. This led to the formation of a financial reserve fund to be used for the amortisation of the public debt through the sales of this national property, the royal chapels and empty benefices, as well as the consequent institutional reform of the Board of Interest of the New Loans, which now assumed powers and duties that belonged to the National Treasury.

The first sign of concern about the subject was shown by the *Cortes Constituintes* in early March 1821, when the parliamentary deputy Francisco António dos Santos presented a proposal for the amortisation of the public debt, through which 'the nation takes responsibility for the public debt, for which the national property and assets constitute a special mortgage' (Santos 1821, 211). This deputy and merchant operating in the Lisbon market based his analysis on a very negative view of Portugal's economic situation, considering the country to have been successively devastated by the French invasions, the English commercial and political domination, and the destruction of the Brazilian trade as a result of the opening up of the ports in 1808 and the free importation of cereals. He considered that it would be possible to establish an amortisation fund through the positive budget balance forecast for 1821. His estimate was that there would be a total income of 7,677,139$368 *réis* and a total expenditure of 7,181,500$000 *réis*. This would provide a positive balance of 495,639$638 *réis*, which would be used primarily for the extinction of paper money.[1] For this purpose, he proposed the establishment of a national bank, which is to be considered as the first demonstration by the *Cortes Constituintes* of the intention to create an institution of this type.

The general tone of the public debate on these matters was one of great apprehension, revealing a sense of national emergency. For the magistrate Sousa Moniz, it was urgent to identify the State's creditors and debtors, stressing that 'the people want to see the national credit redeemed; without this measure being established, the nation will never be able to flourish' (Moniz 1820, 3). Full attention should be given to debtors who were not insolvent and who could legitimately be expected to pay off their debts. In order to achieve this, Moniz proposed that their properties should be pledged or mortgaged. As far as the State's creditors were concerned, he suggested that the amount owed should be discounted by 10 per cent, thus forcing bondholders to withhold some of their invested funds. Finally, he suggested that the State should diversify its sources for financing debt repayment through the sale of chapels, commanderies and ecclesiastical benefices, the public auctioning of uncultivated land and hunting grounds, and the creation of a special tax on urban buildings, varying according to the number of doors and windows that they had (or, in other words, according to their floor space). The political climate created by the liberal revolution allowed for the presentation of solutions that involved a criticism (and ultimately the loss) of the privileges held by members of the *ancien régime*'s social orders.

The solution by means of taxation policies, thus providing the State with an increase in revenues for debt repayment, met with the approval of another participant in this public debate, as conveyed in a pamphlet written and published in December 1820 (Pinto 1820). The *Cortes* (or parliament) was not yet assembled, and therefore the suggestions that this pamphlet contained were addressed to the government, particularly regarding the allocation of existing taxes (property transfer taxes, the ecclesiastical tithe, the water tax and various customs duties) to the amortisation of debt securities.

The question of the State's fiscal capacity was clearly expressed in the opinions aired in the public sphere, and it proved to be crucial for determining the possibility of the State's fulfilling its obligations to administer the public finances, not only in the eyes of the taxpayers, but also, and above all, in the eyes of the holders of debt securities, whose validity the State had, in practice, ceased to recognise. In the words of António José Pedroso de Almeida, the matter was a source of great concern since it affected the very stability of the new political order under construction:

> The administration of the public treasury is the mainstay, the firmest of all supports for governments and one of the safe drivers of the prosperity of states. When it is bad and out of control, it is the cause of all revolutions, the origin of public misery, and the certain ruin of the political machine. . . . What has caused, causes and will cause political revolutions is, above all, the shortage of money, it is the mismanagement of the public treasury.
>
> (Almeida 1822, 3)

This concern with the good organisation of the system of public finances was part of an approach that called for a differentiation to be made of the attributes of a system of liberal government, and therefore a non-absolute one, based on 'frankness, and the publicity that is given to its transactions' (*Projeto ou Memória* 1821, 3). For the anonymous author of this text, it was fundamental to guarantee an adequate administration of income and expenditure, paying special attention to the care that was to be taken in applying public funds and to the technical procedures of double-entry bookkeeping. About the need for the State not to realise expenditures that would bring no useful results to the public, he quoted J.-B. Say's *A Treatise on Political Economy*:

> To administer what should be left to oneself is to harm the governed, and to make them pay for the harm done to them, as if it were good (*Administrer ce qui devrait être abandonné à soi-même, c'est faire du mal aux administrés, et leur faire payer le mal qu'on leur fait, comme si c'était un bien.*
>
> (*Projeto ou Memória* 1821,13)

The theme also mobilised merchants and manufacturers, as was the case with Francisco Gomes Veloso de Azevedo, who published two pamphlets in 1822 dedicated to the subject of discounting paper money (Azevedo 1822a and 1822b). In one of these pamphlets, he proposed technical measures that would prevent the counterfeit issue of paper money and allow for the replacement of old paper bonds with new ones (*apólices*). In this way, the State needed to be rigorously aware of the number of debt securities that should be redeemed and could define a tax-guaranteed plan for the allocation of funds. For this trader operating in the sector of the manufacture and printing of cotton textiles,

> All men are more given to enjoying something, rather than waiting. And so, all of the State's creditors impatiently desire to be paid, either in part or in full. And the more their impatience grows, the greater is their expectation and hope of improvement, which everyone conceived as a consequence of the nation's political regeneration.
>
> (Azevedo 1822a, 6)

The message could not be clearer: State creditors kept hoping that the revolution initiated in 1820 would resolve the default situation in which the State found itself, paying off the public debt and its interest. It was vital that the State should gain the confidence of the holders of debt securities and maintain its good reputation with the political body of the nation. The creation of a climate of trust, in relation to both the debt system and the monetary system, was crucial for the authors participating in this public debate. Although they did not explicitly say so, this positioning revealed the understanding of a fundamental link between high levels of confidence on the part of economic agents and the possibilities of economic development.[2]

The State's creditors were given the choice of transforming their loans into 'irredeemable bonds' that would last forever more, with no redemption date, and which would earn a perpetual interest of 3 per cent per year, or into fixed-term 'redeemable bonds', bearing 4 per cent interest during the period established for their amortisation. Azevedo described in some detail the way in which the payment of interest would be operationalised and the process for the amortisation of the bonds, also adding a lottery project with the aim of obtaining funds to accelerate the sequence of such amortisation operations.

Interestingly, the positioning of this businessman revealed his principled distrust of the reputation of any government, but, at the same time, he felt forced to voice his opinion about a matter that was prejudicial to a significant number of private creditors looking for a solution which would satisfy all parties and provide the State with the indispensable guarantees of public credibility.

The defence of the interests of the State's creditors was the main concern underlying the 1821 proposal of Filipe Arnaud de Medeiros, a lawyer from the *Casa da Suplicação* (the High Court of Appeal) representing a group of aggrieved parties demanding payment of the State's debt to them. The plan that he presented for the redemption of securities would involve the issue of

> three or four million *apólices*, of at least 50 and 100$000, not bearing any interest and with a representative value in accordance with the law; with credit and circulation in all contracts; and in all tax offices; to be used immediately for the redemption and progressive amortisation of some resources, which could be deployed without damage to the Exchequer's current revenues.
>
> (Medeiros 1820a, 7)

The resources that he considered to be necessary for the future amortisation of the new debt issued without any compensation in terms of revenue included the income from vacant ecclesiastical benefices, estates that had no owners, and the profits resulting from the extinction of some entails, chapels and brotherhoods.

Curiously, this proposal was immediately and publicly refuted by an anonymous author, who protested about the attitude of rejection displayed towards paper money, explaining that the problem did not lie in its existence, but instead in the successive mistakes that had been made since it had first begun to circulate in 1796, evoking the teachings of political economy on this subject:

> As you very well know, paper money is useful in a State, and, instead of being its ruin, it can increase its opulence, amplifying its representative signs, if those who are at the head of its finances know how to deal with it, and believe in it. This is what we are taught in the classes that we both attend, and what we are taught by the good economists, whose principles and lessons I think that you still remember.
>
> (*Refutação* 1820, 4)

This refutation of the proposal did not go unanswered, with Arnaud de Medeiros once again coming to the defence of his cause. On this occasion, he published an article in the newspaper *Mnemosine Constitucional*, offering an eloquent exemplification of the public debate that had been opened up immediately after the uprisings of August and September 1820 (Medeiros 1820b).

The discounting of paper money in circulation served as a crucial argument in demonstrating the need for public confidence in the institutions that had emerged from the 1820 revolution (*Memória* 1821). Replacing the bonds (*apólices*) in circulation with new paper securities accredited by the Board of Interest, and honouring the commitments to the payment of interest, were essential measures for re-establishing the State's credibility. The revenue required for the realisation of this plan would come from the vacant ecclesiastical benefices and chapels, from the collection of ecclesiastical income and from the sale of national property. According to this anonymous author:

> In order to destroy the discounting of paper money, it is enough to comply fully with the law of its creation, establishing sufficient public revenue for the payment of its interest, whose payment must be made with the greatest possible exactness, facility and publicity, and the secret consists in convincing the public that it will always be done in this way and without any inviolability.
>
> (*Memória* 1821, 20)

An identical position about the sources of the revenue that was indispensable for conducting this type of operation of redeeming paper money was upheld by Diogo Ratton (1821), who insisted, in particular, on the choice of the Board of Interest as the institution responsible for the exchange of old *apólices* and their replacement with new paper securities bearing 5 per cent interest, with such a function remaining independent of the public Treasury (the Royal Exchequer).

Besides these rhetorical proclamations, it was essential to take care of the practical procedures that would allow for the removal from circulation of the devalued paper money.

> A friend that I hold in some esteem tells me that when he reads the *Diário do Governo* and finds in it pompous declarations about our regeneration, he

> normally casts a glance at the price of discounting paper money. Which is stated at the end of these same pages.
>
> (*Memória* 1821, 12)

One of the most interesting projects about these themes was published anonymously under the monogram *F.J.C.F. Constitutional Citizen* (1821), in which its author proposed a 25 per cent increase in the value of the gold coins in circulation, achieved through the handing in of paper money without any discount or rebate, which would then be promptly burned in full view of its owner. This would not only serve as a stimulus for the retention of gold currency, preventing it from leaving the country, but also lead to the progressive elimination of paper money without the inconvenience associated with its rebate.

For some of the political journalists involved in these debates, the problem of the discredited nature of paper money was almost an obsession, leading them to insist on its rapid or progressive extinction, but without taking the care to present alternative solutions for monetary circulation, as is clear from the texts written by José Ezequiel da Costa Ricci (1820), José Joaquim Bordalo (1821) and an author identified only by his initials (A.T.C.S. 1822). Particularly interesting was a text written by Manuel Rodrigues Lucas de Sena (1821), with the suggestive and militant title of *Papel moeda fora* (Get rid of paper money), although this was never published. In this text, he presented the bold but impractical proposal of an extraordinary tax of 5 per cent on the value of the property of roughly half of the Portuguese population, which would be valid for the period of 1 year and would be used to create a fund necessary for the amortisation of the paper money in circulation.

More realistic, however, were the projects that were published, and which made an explicit reference to the need for a bank as an institution geared towards the management of two main problems that affected the credibility of the State, namely the non-fulfilment of the commitments arising from the public debt and the lack of control over fiduciary circulation. One of the most important texts on this subject was published by an anonymous author, who signed himself as 'a Portuguese', who estimated the value of the paper money in circulation at 10 million *cruzados* and who considered that 'the creation of paper money was the most disastrous blow delivered by financial ignorance' (*Considerações importantes* 1821, 5). Displaying his disagreement with the ideas and proposals under discussion in the public sphere – namely the already-mentioned plan of Costa Ricci – this anonymous 'Portuguese' proposed the formation of a fund to be used for the amortisation of paper money through the creation of a

> national bank, which would exclusively occupy itself with this branch of activity and that of the public debt, although it would, however, be completely independent of the public treasury, and the executive power, since such dependence has always caused the ruin of similar establishments.
>
> (*Considerações importantes* 1821, 22)

Among the various pamphlets published at the time, it is worth mentioning Vicente Cardoso da Costa's curious proposal for the creation of a bank specifically designed for overseeing the process of public debt management (Costa 1822). The author acknowledged from the start that, due to an unexpected delay in its publication, his proposal had lost its political momentum, since the *Cortes* had already approved the constitution of the Bank of Lisbon. But the problem he was discussing did not fail to give rise to contributions that kept people thinking about the role of a bank in the new constitutional political conjuncture.

Costa's main concern was to reactivate what he considered to be a 'stalled circulation' that prevented a normal relationship between sellers and buyers in the market.

> Money is the vehicle of circulation; it is the cart on which it walks and drives. It is currently lacking; therefore, the only remedy is to make it appear: and the circulation banks are in this case the only remedy that one can make use of. Its notes will return to the public as a cash amount, which will go into circulation, since other one that previously served has since disappeared.
>
> (Costa 1822, 9)

The difficulty of finding shareholders for such a venture could be resolved by resorting to holders of public debt through the conversion of their interest-bearing debt securities (large *apólices*) into the bank's capital. In this way, the former public debt would be extinguished and the new capital would appreciate thanks to the bank's income-generating operations. Shareholders would therefore receive an interest payment (corresponding to the debt securities converted into shares) and dividends, based on the results of the bank's operations and the number of shares that they held. The author admitted that he did not know the exact amount of the former public debt, which was why he did not mention the amount of the capital that would be needed to set up the bank. However, the important point to be borne in mind here is the clearly innovative nature of this subscription procedure.

This National Bank would be able to issue notes that replaced the devalued paper money, with the bank itself managing the extinction of the previous paper money that it would accept to buy below its nominal value and without payment of any interest. The gains from this operation would be channelled into a state loan fund. In order to begin its operations, a bullion fund would be set up through the sale of 'national buildings'. The bank would discount bills of exchange and short-term loans at a 4 per cent interest rate. Costa's intention was to give the bank an instrumental role in the process of wealth creation: 'This moderate interest will encourage and aid agriculture, manufactures and commercial enterprises, for the benefit of public wealth and prosperity' (Costa 1822, 20).

Costa gave special attention to the need to distinguish between different types of fiduciary circulation (paper money issued by the State and banknotes issued by a private bank). Furthermore, he warned of the inflationary risks of an excessive monetary circulation (mainly in the form of banknotes) and asked for a rigorous selection of qualified people for the bank's management. Finally, we should note Cardoso da Costa's insistence on a political dimension that was not always made explicit in the technical literature on financial and banking matters: the bank rendered a service to the Constitution, the State and the regeneration movement, so that the Constitution and the State therefore had to repay and compensate the bank for the importance of its mission.

> We consider that the establishment of this bank is not only extremely profitable, but also a condition, *sine qua non*, for happily progressing towards our political regeneration: we do not regard it as constitutional, that is to say, as a necessary support for the Constitution. The Constitution will support the bank, and this will do as much in return. As it will be possible for the public spirit to be conserved with the necessary firmness by the new institutions, if the State's paper credit weakens instead of improving! If the great and most useful class of citizens who live from their daily work becomes more unhappy, without having anyone to offer them employment, instead of their condition appearing to be more plentiful and fortunate! If, because of the very low prices of things, all agricultural and industrial products begin to depreciate day by day, making it impossible for these enterprises, such genuine sources of public wealth, to continue to work!
>
> (Costa 1822, 21)

The contents of these proposals and messages were extended to other areas of the public sphere, particularly in the newspapers dedicated to reporting the national and international political situation, which had proliferated in Lisbon and Porto since September 1820. The theme of public credit and debt repayment was widely discussed in various newspapers, which insisted in particular on calling for the payments that were owed to private creditors. Accompanying the public debate on technical solutions relating to the debt amortisation process, the newspapers opened their pages to the collaboration of authors who rejected the published proposals or reported the public debates dedicated to this problem. This was the case with the already-mentioned *Mnemosine Constitucional* (written by Pedro Alexandre Cravoé) and *O Liberal* (edited by António Maria do Couto), which published small items of news about the circulation of paper money and the initial version of the text by Costa Ricci (1820), which would later be published as an autonomous pamphlet.

The same tone of concern about the State's failure to fulfil its obligations was evident in the testimony of José Liberato Freire de Carvalho, the main editor of the *Campeão Português em Lisboa ou o Amigo do Povo e do Rei Constitucional* (Carvalho 1822), who opened the pages of his newspaper to authors who anonymously sent him their ideas about the way in which the State could honour its commitments to paying the public debt (I.F.P.B. 1822).

A special mention should be made of the *Jornal da Sociedade Literária e Patriótica*, which published two important articles discussing the question of public debt and public credit. In the first of these articles, the editor Nuno Pato Moniz defined public credit as follows:

> Public credit is the cornerstone of all social buildings: it consists in the government precisely and religiously fulfilling all of its contracts; in paying its employees regularly, and its debts to the letter and on a certain day, or in fulfilling the promises that it has undertaken; in guaranteeing the safety and security of individuals and property; and, in a word, public credit is the trust that each person has in the government's promises.
>
> (Moniz 1822, 42)

He noted that the government that had emerged from the liberal revolution of 1820 had shown itself to be incapable of resolving and repaying the internal loan that had been taken out at the end of the eighteenth century and, perhaps even more seriously, it had not succeeded in establishing the levels of trust and confidence that would enable it to take out a new internal public loan, which was, however, absolutely essential for helping to meet the payments that were due to the public servants. Given the urgency of the situation, the writer of this article proposed that the possible realisation of such a loan should be accompanied by a process of consolidation of the pre-existing public debt and the payment of the respective interest, asking the creditors to trust in the constitutional government and the new political situation, which offered conditions providing a safe guarantee that the State would fulfil its obligations. The social consequences resulting from the delays in payments were regarded as a serious political risk that could endanger the population's support for the cause of the so-called regeneration.

In another article published in the same newspaper, a transcription was made of a debate that had taken place at the *Sociedade Literária e Patriótica*, with the participation of some of its members who would later perform important roles in the national political and financial life, such as Paulo Midosi, Carlos Morato Roma and Mouzinho da Silveira. After an initial presentation by Carlos Morato Roma of the factors involved in sustaining and supporting the public credit, those taking part in the debate spoke about the advantages and disadvantages of having a theoretical knowledge of political economy in order to be able to reply to the question of knowing whether it would be possible or advisable to make a loan to the State. The replies that were given were different and the minutes that were taken of the meeting show that the debate was particularly intense. However, the prevailing opinion was that a position of prudence should be adopted in the administration of the public finance system, given the situation of low confidence or the distrust of private individuals in the State's capacity to be able to honour its commitments.

The testimony left by Mouzinho da Silveira revealed his extreme fear of increasing the debt, considering that the solution would have to be that of making a significant cut in public spending:

> What trust can there be in a government whose Treasury spends more than it receives? If the revenue is less than the expenditure, then there needs to be an amendment, and this can only be to increase the revenue or lessen the expenditure: for many reasons, we cannot count on an increase in revenue. Mainly because of the state of uncertainty in which we find ourselves with regard to Brazil: let us therefore turn our attention to the expenditure, which must be reduced immediately and as much as possible: cuts can be made either through a general reduction, or by eliminating gracious pensions, free wages, etc.: both of these things seem fair to me.
>
> (Silveira 1822, 707)

Carlos Morato Roma was similarly not very keen on the loan, but he left up in the air the inevitability of resorting to a new debt issue, in view of the seriousness of the situation that the country was now facing.

> Although many economists with great reputations have striven to show that the use of public credit is useful for all states, it is my opinion that those who believe that it is always prejudicial, except when it can be used to increase public revenue, or when the State finds itself in such circumstances that the same may be said about it as is said of a building that is beginning to burn, namely that it is necessary to demolish a part of it in order to save the rest. As Portugal perhaps finds itself almost in this latter case, I am not far from considering a loan to be convenient; provided that it is taken from national capitalists, since only in extreme circumstances should it be taken from foreigners, and only after all other recourses have been exhausted should we make use of this heroic remedy, which may condemn the patient to the grave much sooner.
>
> (Roma 1822, 437)

The solution of resorting to the credit provided by national capitalists implicitly pointed to the recognition of the role to be played by the Bank of Lisbon, as will be discussed later on.

Among the various periodical newspapers that made a dramatic appearance immediately after the revolution of 1820, one in particular stood out from the rest because of the quality and frequency of the texts that it devoted to economic and financial matters. This was the case with *O Independente*, edited by two of the main protagonists of the regeneration movement that began in 1820, Manuel Fernandes Tomás and José Joaquim Ferreira de Moura. It was precisely in the pages of *O Independente* that articles were published that were more favourable to the idea of taking out a loan due to the urgent need to meet the payments owing to the public servants, as confirmed by the following excerpt from an anonymous collaborator:

> I shall conclude, Editor, that the public servants cannot be paid regularly without a loan; the State cannot profitably purchase what it needs to maintain its establishments, and, humanly speaking, it cannot consolidate our glorious regeneration. So, we must resort immediately to a loan; because it is the remedy, or the last hope of salvation, to which the nations that best know their interests have always resorted in great crises.
>
> (Epiménides 1822, 397)

The solution for the loan lay in the involvement of the Bank of Lisbon, whose formation at the *Cortes* had been accompanied by the editors of *O Independente*, who had expressed their support for such an initiative in the pages of their newspaper, justifying the ample privileges that should be granted to their shareholders (Moura and Tomás 1821), and revealing their concern with the initially weak mobilisation of the capitalists available for the subscription of the bank's capital (Moura and Tomás 1822). The range of their interventions in the public sphere will be easier to understand after we have accompanied the contents of the parliamentary speeches that they made in the debates leading to the decree of the creation of the Bank of Lisbon.

## 4.2 Budget and deficit: constitutional and political framework

Before taking a closer look at the process of the creation of the Bank of Lisbon, it is important to gain a better understanding of the political essence of the problem at stake, or, in other words, the state of the kingdom's public finances, which reveals a growing deficit between the State's collection of its revenue and the level of its spending.

The debates taking place in the press, at the parliament and in the public sphere, highlight the importance of searching for solutions to problems that obviously did not arise because of the regeneration movement. However, they also show that the rhetorical emphasis in what was a supposedly calamitous situation for the public accounts did not correspond in any way to the reality, as revealed by the available quantitative indicators. The crucial question was, after all, the State's credibility in terms of its management of a consolidated debt that, despite the fact that it had remained reasonably stable throughout the first two decades of the nineteenth century, proved to be a heavy burden for the expectations that the political and economic agents were forming about its future evolution.

The historiographical works that have formed the basis for subsequent studies about the public finances in Portugal in the first decades of the nineteenth century point to a negative balance between effective revenue and expenditure, whose origins dated back to the late eighteenth century and could be explained by the increase in military spending associated with the Portuguese army's participation in the defence against the hegemonic pretensions of the French and Spanish (the campaigns of Roussillon and Catalonia, the War of the Oranges, the French Invasions). This deficit gradually began to decrease and was finally eliminated in 1812, once the French defeat in Portugal had been consummated. Equilibrium was maintained only very briefly, giving rise once again to an increase in State spending, supposedly resulting from the British demands regarding the budgetary allocation for the defence of the territory (Silveira 1987, Pinheiro 1991 and Caetano 2006). Recent studies based on a new quantitative approach to the study of the State's income and expenditure (using data taken from the Ledgers of Current Income and Expenditure of the Paymaster-General of the Royal Exchequer, *Arquivo Histórico do Tribunal de Contas*) show that a situation of equilibrium was maintained between effective revenue and expenditure. This was because of a substantial part of the military expenses incurred during the Napoleonic wars were offset by the British aid that was not recorded in the Exchequer's accounts (Caetano 2013).

However, regardless of the calculation of the deficit that may be made today, at the time in question, the issue that remained on the agenda was the management of the public debt created in order to meet the increase in State spending. Given the impossibility of making an overly complex structure for the collection of revenue profitable, and, in view of the manifest lack of opportunities for launching new taxes, the solutions that were chosen for the financing of public spending were based on the creation of internal public debt, the founding moment of which was the first loan of 4,000 *contos* made available in November 1796. From then until 1820, there was a succession of other operations for the reinforcement and consolidation of the debt, which gave rise to the enormous tension between the State's needs and obligations. Its reputation stained by its failure to amortise the debt securities (*apólices*) and to meet the interest payments, the State accumulated various motives for discontent among its creditors, as was explained earlier. The pioneering solutions for the consolidation and redemption of the debt proposed by Dom Rodrigo de Sousa Coutinho (between 1796 and 1803) had not been taken any further or had had only a very limited scope, as was the case with the sale of crown property between 1810 and 1820, which raised the small amount of 439 *contos*, or, in other words, roughly 2 per cent of the amount of the consolidated debt in the 3-year period of the liberal revolution, normally referred to as *vintismo* (Tengarrinha 1993).

The path to be followed in achieving the much-desired restructuring of the now constitutional kingdom's public finances was not an easy one. But there were some promising signs, at the merely formal and programmatic level, which were clearly established in the texts of the Constitution (*Constituição* 1822) and the Constitutional Charter (*Carta Constitucional* 1826). Thus, in the chapter about the tasks of the *Cortes*, a definition is provided on the prerogatives of the legislative power, which were to

> annually fix taxes and public expenditure, . . . authorise the government to take out loans, . . . establish suitable means for the payment of the public debt, . . . regulate the administration of national property and decree its sale in the event of necessity, . . . and create or suppress public jobs or offices.
>
> (Article 103, §s IX to XIII of the Constitution)

An identical formulation was adopted on these same matters in the Constitutional Charter (Article 15, §s 8, 11, 12, 13 and 14).

In the chapter dedicated to the government's tasks, in the section relating to the national treasury, both the constitutional texts defined the executive's powers in the collection of revenue and the administration of expenditure, and the respective surveillance, as well as in the management of the public debt. And they established the obligation of the annual presentation by the Secretary of State for the Treasury of the budget of expected revenue and expenditure and the general account of the revenue and expenditure in the previous year (Articles 224–236 of the Constitution; articles 75, §13 and 136 to 138 of the Constitutional Charter).

In its general provisions and guarantees of the civil and political rights of Portuguese citizens, the Constitutional Charter of 1826 also established the duty to contribute to the State's expenditure, in proportion to the property of each person (Article 145, §14), and recognised and guaranteed the existing public debt (Article 145, §22).

The theoretical understanding of public finances according to the modern liberal conception was systematised in a pioneering fashion by José Ferreira Borges in the following terms:

> Taxation is the contribution of the subjects of a nation, imposed by its legitimate representatives, with the aim of enabling the government to make the expenditure necessary to ensure compliance with the law, and the national security and prosperity.
>
> (Borges 1831, 1)

This amounted to a recognition that the State's financial system is founded on the voluntary sacrifice that each person freely makes in order to achieve the property and benefits resulting from the judicious and supervised application of the expenditure made by the State on behalf of society as a whole. The claim that the taxation system should be universal and in adequacy to the income of each taxpayer, as well as the care that is taken in guaranteeing that the tax requirements do not penalise the sources for the creation of wealth, were just some of the classical ideas of the political economy of taxation that Ferreira Borges handled in such an accessible and pedagogical manner.

In this way, we can recognise that the formal procedures relating to the establishment of a doctrinal framework for the State's new financial system were duly taken care of at the constitutional and political levels. However, it should also be pointed out that the political unrest that continued to be experienced until the end of the civil war of 1832–34 did not always make it possible for the constitutional precepts and theoretical principles to have the desired outcome in matters of budgetary policy relating to the collection of government revenue and tax reform, the administration of expenditure and its functional distribution, the taking out of internal and external loans and the management of the floating, funded and special debt.[3]

Table 4.1 gives us a rough idea of the budgetary imbalance in the period 1820–28. It is an 'approximate idea' because the information collected is based on sources from that time of a budgetary nature, which do not show us with great exactness the effective results of the State general account.

The amounts recorded here make it possible to understand how the presentation of budgets at the *Cortes* expressed the need to discuss the policies associated with the management of the budget deficit, which was clearly the crucial problem, requiring solutions that would inevitably increase indebtedness. Although the budgets were not subject to any formal general voting, the intense discussions and partial votes on the items of expenditure of the various ministries, as well as on the revenue resulting from the collection of taxes, show that there had been a complete break from the secret and arbitrary nature of the decisions that were previously taken about the State's financial affairs.

First of all, it should be noted that (according to the sources of that time) the information relating to the period 1815–19 shows that there was a budgetary surplus, in contrast to the customarily held negative view of the State's financial situation. This is a question that justifies further investigation in the future, in order to confirm the theory suggesting that the non-inclusion of the English

*Table 4.1* Budgets of the Liberal Revolution, 1820–34 (in *contos*)

| *Year* | *Revenue* | *Expenditure* | *Balance* | *Source* |
|---|---|---|---|---|
| 1815–1819 (annual average) | 9,759 | 9,719 | +40 | M. Silveira 1826–1828, 1095 Pinto 1839, 69 |
| 1820–1823 (annual average) | 7,735 | 10,584 | −2,849 | M. Silveira 1826–1828, 1095 |
| 1826–1828 (annual average) | 7,489 | 9,790 | −2,301 | M. Silveira 1826-1828, 219 |
| 1821 (budget) | 7,677 | 8,519 | −842 | *DC*, 10 March 1821, 243 |
| 1822 (budget) | 7,232 | 8,839 | −1,607 | Pinto 1839, 71 |
| 1823 (budget) | 7,734 | 12,000* | −4,266 | *DC*, 1 February. 1823, 663 |
| 1826 (budget) | 8,860 | 11,356 | −2,496 | Franzini 1827, 72 |
| 1827 (budget) | 7,495 | 9,941 | −2,446 | Pinto 1839, 72 |
| 1828 (budget) | 11,031 | 15,257 | −4,226 | Pinto 1839, 73 |

*Estimate extrapolated from the sectoral values of the expenses approved at the *Cortes* (*DC*, February and March, 1823)

military aid in the national accounts helps to explain the good performance of the public finances in the period before 1820 (Moreira, Reis and Sousa 2021).

As there is not enough space here to engage in a detailed analysis of the budgets presented at the *Cortes* for each year that the parliament was assembled, we shall just take a few examples that may help to explain the State's financial policy, beginning with the illustrative case of the first budget relating to the year 1821.[4] A large share of the estimated revenue was represented by the income from customs duties (36.5 per cent) and the tobacco contract (18.5 per cent), demonstrating some continuity with regard to the situation before 1820. A certain rigidity in the structure of revenue was to be confirmed throughout the period, revealing a serious difficulty in implementing a tax reform that would enable the revenue to be adapted to the needs of the liberal State (Reis 1996, 41–43). An enormous part of the expenditure was to be explained by the spending on the army and navy (representing two-thirds of total expenses), requiring the mobilisation of 73.5 per cent of the volume of revenue stored in the public coffers in order to be paid in its entirety. Such an enormous volume of expenditure justified the apprehension displayed by the Public Finance Committee, which recommended measures to reduce this item or else the inevitable recourse to a loan in order to bear these costs.

In the debate on the budget that marked the end of the 3-year liberal period (between February and March 1823), there was an intensification of the concern about the spending cuts that would imply drastic decreases in activity and urgent institutional reforms, or even the closure of official bodies that would not have any correspondence in the new constitutional political environment (Pinheiro 1991, 55–58). In this sense, it is easy to understand the critical tone of the members of parliament in relation to the excessive spending of institutions such as the House of Bragança, the Patriarchal See, the Royal College of Nobles, the *Mesa da Consciência e Ordens* (Board of the King's Conscience and of the Military Orders), the Inquisition Tribunal (which, although it had been suppressed, still continued to process expenditure), as well as in relation to the superfluous building work being conducted at the Palácio da Ajuda, or the organisational chaos of the Public Treasury. However, it is interesting to note the inclusion of the Royal Printing Office, the Botanical Garden and the Lisbon Academy of Sciences in the list of institutions that merited the disapproval of the most intransigent members of parliament in matters relating to budgetary restrictions. The institutions of a cultural and scientific nature did not escape the efforts to introduce greater budgetary restraint that were considered an urgent political priority. Shortly afterwards, however, the absolutist uprising (*Vilafrancada*) would render the continued parliamentary discussion of these and any other treasury matters impracticable.

A third important period was the one before the return of Dom Miguel to Portugal and his acclamation as the absolute king, or, in other words, before the sudden and abrupt end to the ordinary legislature that had been initiated in October 1826. In the preliminary report presented to the *Cortes* at its session on 11 February 1828, the Minister of the Treasury, Manuel António de

Carvalho, was far from supposing that the careful reflections about the estimated revenue and expenditure for 1828 – including the summarised account of the revenue and expenditure of the Public Treasury for 1827, the account of the revenue and expenditure of the Board of Interest for the same year and the approximate budget of the State's public debt for the year 1828 – would end up being of no consequence. But the synthetic testimony that he presented to the Chamber of Deputies clearly reveals the difficulties of systematically organising the information that was necessary for knowing the state of the Treasury:

> In order to arrive, Gentlemen, at such a useful result, it is necessary for the Treasury to organise itself in accordance with the terms set out in the Charter; for it to practise a simple, methodical and judiciously classified form of bookkeeping; and for the same organisation to be given to all the establishments of public administration, whichever they may be, so that everything can proceed to its end in a harmonious fashion and so that the desired result can be easily obtained.
>
> (*DC*, 11 February 1828, 427)

The gradual increase of the budget deficit (and of the State general account) and the recognition of the difficulty of introducing new taxes or significantly reducing the State's expenditure, made it ever more urgent to resort to internal and external loans to meet the State's financing requirements.[5] In fact, it was precisely in this context that the pressing need to fund the deficit of the State's finances was revealed, with the creation of a banking institution geared towards such a purpose being regarded as inevitable. Such was the requirement that positioned the Bank of Lisbon at the centre of the political debate at the *Cortes Constituintes* of 1821–22, as well as at the *Cortes Ordinárias* of 1822–23 and 1826–28, focusing on the questions of the budget deficit and the public debt. Let us now return to the parliamentary debate that lay at the origin of the creation of the Bank of Lisbon.

## 4.3 The Public Finance Committee and the solution of a public bank

The *Cortes Constituintes* and its specialised committees also received many expressions of concern about the state of the country in a wide range of areas, naturally including the domain of public credit and the credibility of the financial institutions. In the years 1821 and 1822, the Public Finance Committee received a total of 63 reports and opinions about the financial situation, in addition to some 332 letters and petitions relating to the private problems of citizens and institutions who complained of tax evasion, abuses of power and breaches of contract, or who claimed rights and benefits facilitated by the new political situation. Amongst the reports whose content was of the greatest analytical interest, the most noteworthy were the observations and proposals on the circulation of paper money, the amortisation of public debt, the elimination or creation of new taxes and, in general, on problems relating to the reform of the system for the administration of public finance.[6]

The contents of these reports did not always display any particularly impressive explanatory quality or any great rigour in their analysis of the problems to which some anonymous or common citizens drew the attention of the members of the *Cortes Constituintes*. The proposals that they made were mainly concerned with the redemption of the paper money in circulation and its replacement by new *apólices* duly certified by the Public Treasury or the Ministry of Finance. The main justification for this request was to reduce the losses for the private holders of paper money, whose devaluation (in relation to the initial value of its issue as debt securities) was estimated to range between 20 and 25 per cent on average, although there were reports of discounts amounting to as much as roughly 40 per cent. Equally important was the concern with guaranteeing the regularity of the payments to the public servants, for which fiduciary money could not be used without its value being duly guaranteed by the State. In this context, the creation of funds through an internal loan or the raising of extraordinary revenues obtained through the public auction of vacant ecclesiastical benefices were measures that were regarded as 'a necessary means of sustaining the credit that our finances are seeking so hard, the only bulwark to consolidate the constitutional system' (Anonymous 1821).

Generally speaking, these proposals sent to the Public Finance Committee did not display any great novelty compared to the contents of the texts written with greater formal care and superior analytical relevance that, as has already been said, were circulating in printed form, during that same period, among a much wider public audience. In their anxiety to gain greater publicity, and thus hoping for a prompt acceptance, some citizens caused their previously printed plans to be sent directly to the Parliamentary Committees. This was the case, for example, with João da Mata Milheiro, who proposed setting up a fund for the amortisation of paper money through the imposition of new taxes on the consumption of imported luxury goods (such as tea, cinnamon, pepper and tobacco). This fund would be managed by two boards of traders to be set up in Porto and Lisbon, which would be responsible for collecting paper money and replacing it with new and duly accredited fiduciary securities (Milheiro 1821).

However, despite the public recognition that certain deputies were gaining for themselves at the parliamentary sessions, the members of the Public Finance Committee only sporadically showed any signs that they were paying attention to these spontaneous interlocutors. One curious case was the annotation that was made on an anonymous petition or 'complaints against the abandonment of paper money to the detriment of the public', in which this clearly minority position in defence of paper currency was opposed by an opinion of the Public Finance Committee, who explained that 'the author of this petition wishes that citizens be obliged to always receive paper in their agreements to pay any debts of real amounts', using and quoting the authority of the argument of Jean-Baptiste Say in order to underline the unjust nature of such a claim.[7]

As was inevitable, the question of creating a banking institution was addressed in many of these texts, as, for example, in the proposals presented to the Public Finance Committee by José Joaquim Freire (1821) and by João Carlos de Vam (1821), who expressly associated the aim of amortising paper money with the institutional instrument that was indispensable for producing such an effect. In some cases, the authors of the texts directly invoked the hopes and expectations being nurtured about the advantages that the new liberal regime would bring. As one of the proponents of the creation of a bank wrote: 'Lisbon, which today is fortunate enough to have a representative national government, should seize the opportunity and take full advantage of it' (Gallard 1821, 4).

The importance given to the factors and conditions that made the design of new political and institutional solutions possible is clearly demonstrated in the following excerpt from another proponent of the creation of a bank who submitted his idea to the appreciation of the Public Finance Committee:

> There is no disputing the legitimacy of the power that the *Cortes* of this Kingdom currently enjoys, as the General Council of the Nation, to reform finances, and to adopt the system for the administration of public revenue that is the smoothest and most advantageous to the State. Any fundamental laws that this nation has finally decided to embrace will never cease to conform absolutely to all decisions, since they are recognised by the current ministry to be favourable to national interests, and, as such, are authorised to have their due effect.
>
> (Jordão 1821, 22)

Besides new proposals, the Public Finance Committee also welcomed old suggestions that had been forgotten or that had previously been considered inadmissible. A good example is the proposal for a *Banco de Socorro* (Support Bank), which João Henriques Sequeira again presented in April 1821, and which was identical in every respect to the aforementioned project that he had presented in 1819. In this case, the Public Finance Committee issued an opinion that revealed the attitude of the established powers in relation to those bank projects that did not expressly state the purpose of serving as a bank for the amortisation of the paper money in circulation. It therefore stated:

> The Public Finance Committee feels obliged to declare that the National Treasury does not have sufficient funds to set up the proposed bank. If the bank is useful to the shareholders, and whoever may wish to be so, the Committee not only sees no inconvenience in this happening, but also considers that the public would benefit from such an institution that is well-known in Europe.
>
> (Sequeira 1821)

Or, in other words, the parliament considered it both opportune and useful to create a banking institution that would be promoted by private shareholders, but it was not prepared to guarantee its promoters any favours, since there was no matter of public interest that would justify this.

Some members of parliament showed themselves to be receptive to the idea of creating a 'national bank established by a society of capitalist businessmen, in which the government would have no influence other than being able to give it that portion that it would be interested in having' (Santos 1821, 212). Or, in other words, according to the deputy Francisco António dos Santos, who enjoyed close links with business activities in insurance companies, it was essential to find an institutional solution for the amortisation of the public debt, which would involve considering the crown property as national property that could be used as collateral (without, however, being sold) and providing a public incentive for the establishment of a private bank. It should be remembered that this was the first time that the proposal for the establishment of a bank had been formally stated in the *Cortes Constituintes*.

Similar projects were put forward by the deputy Alexandre Gomes Ferrão and by the Regency (*DC* 1821, 239 and 575), who transmitted to parliament the contents of the proposals that they had received for the creation of a national bank in Lisbon. And the deputy Francisco Soares Franco, who was always an influential figure in the discussion of economic and financial matters, also presented his own project that was sent to the Public Finance and Trade Committees. Although it was not possible to find any trace of this in the documentation of the Parliamentary Historical Archive, it was undoubtedly this contribution by Soares Franco that served as the working basis for the drafting of the bank proposal subsequently presented by the Public Finance Committee and discussed at the plenary session of the *Cortes Constituintes* in December 1821 (*DC* 1821, 1682).

## 4.4 A divergent proposal

Among this group of texts submitted for the appreciation of the *Cortes*, it is important to highlight the proposal by João Loureiro, a Lisbon businessman, sent by the deputy José Ferreira Borges for the assessment and opinion of the Trade Committee (DC 1821, 239). Unlike most proposals for the constitution of banks, which were channelled to the Public Finance Committee, João Loureiro's text was considered by the Trade Committee, given the contents of its argumentation. The author spoke about the requirements of a bank that was not planned to solve the problem of the amortisation of the public debt or the redemption of paper money and fiduciary circulation, nor even to serve as a State creditor operating a public loan, but instead to serve as a credit institution granting loans to private citizens and public bodies, with the aim of financing economic activities (Loureiro 1821). Curiously, this bank was also christened by the author of the proposal with the name of the Bank of Lisbon, anticipating the name that would be adopted by the institution to be established later on, even though it had a quite different mission and aims. In view of its different nature, it is worth analysing the content of João Loureiro's project in greater detail.

The proposal consisted of two basic documents, entitled 'Conditions' and 'Bylaws', accompanied by a long and carefully written explanatory note and two formal messages addressed to the deputies of the Trade Committee. The explanatory note sought to justify the relationship between the bank and the public powers, clarifying benefits and privileges that might be construed as abuses of the trust that the State was obliged to attribute to the bank's shareholders. Why were so many precautions considered to be advisable? Undoubtedly because their promoter undervalued the crucial question that was being discussed in the public sphere and at parliament, namely the need for the extinction of paper money, and with it the settlement of the public debt. Albeit in an implicit and somewhat approximate fashion, João Loureiro acknowledged that this was a matter that would be resolved through mechanisms for the self-regulation of the market for the supply and demand of money, so that a solution resulting from the bank's own deliberate actions was not to be expected. In his own words:

> We must not be frightened by the 47 million [*réis*] of paper money that there is, when we all know from our own experience that the purchase of 40 or 30 *contos* of metal in paper money immediately causes its value to fall; and if, on the next day, another 10 or 15 *contos* are purchased, by the third day it is no longer possible to find *contos de réis* for sale, and, moreover, they do not cease to exist: the bank does not need to buy more than two hundred *contos de réis*, or, to explain myself better, the bank does not need to invest anything more than two hundred *contos de réis* in the accreditation of paper money for this to reach par value, and to be sought after for purchases to be made legally; but this same operation must neither be announced, nor must it be felt by the public, and it is for this reason, as my main point is to accredit paper money, that I have not even spoken about it in the whole of my plan.
>
> (Loureiro 1821, 13–14)

In this way, the Bank of Lisbon, which was proposed by João Loureiro, centred its attributes on operations that would promote economic activity, based on the premise that:

> The greater our development in agriculture, trade and industry, and the closer that this development is to taking place, removing the obstacles that we have had so far, the less trouble will be caused for us by that portion of the State's debt that is in paper money.
>
> (Loureiro 1821, 14)

The bank would begin its activity after the subscription of 800 shares of 1 *conto de réis*, with there being no upper limit for the formation of its capital. The bank would be established in such a way as to afford continuity to the role already attributed to the Board of Public Deposit, which would mean collecting and storing a multiplicity of assets in the form of gold, silver and jewels originating from confiscations, pledges and embargos associated with numerous private judgements, including the property of the Office of the Judge of the Orphans, Dead and Absent of the overseas territories. The bank would also take over the role of the Board of Interest, thus earning the right to receive a wide range of tax revenue and rents administered by public institutions.

The directors of the bank, who were to be recruited from among well-to-do businessmen, would gain significant profits from a series of activities that presupposed the loss of benefits for the State, including, most notably, the following: discounting of bills of exchange, customs bills, salaries and wages; granting of risky loans for trade in the ports of Asia and America; loans to public establishments and factories of the kingdom, through the setting up of safe mortgages; acceptance of deposits in bullion, gold, silver, jewels and precious stones; sale of commodities to Brazil without the payment of commissions to the Treasury; auctioning of Treasury contracts; issue of banknotes and purchase of foreign currency. On all of these operations, interest could be charged, ranging from 1 to 6 per cent, depending on the associated risk.[8]

Faced with the prospect of private business that was represented by this Bank of Lisbon as proposed by João Loureiro, it is not surprising that the opinion issued by the Trade Committee and written by José Ferreira Borges would be a negative one:

> It seemed to the Committee that the idea of establishing a credit bank, which has arisen on occasions at this August Congress, would be of advantage for the nation: while the idea was not to be disregarded, nor was it possible not to praise the author of the project, it was, nonetheless, impossible to accept his plan, because it was extremely complicated and encompassed objects, transactions and privileges that would be extraneous to other similar establishments.
>
> (Loureiro 1821, 1)

## 4.5 Final details in the proposal for a public bank

It was in this environment favouring a parliamentary debate on the subject that the Minister of the Treasury, José Inácio da Costa, presented a report to the Sovereign Congress in which he sought to answer the following preliminary questions that had been expressly addressed to him by José Ferreira Borges (*DC* 1821, 2523): What was the reason for the increase in the discounting of paper money? And what was the remedy for lessening or destroying this evil? (Costa 1821). In the answers that he gave to parliament, he made it clear that the aim was to pursue the purpose (so frequently attempted but never actually achieved) of creating an 'absolutely private' bank, operating in harmony with economic policy measures that should not be limited to the monetary and financial sphere, indicating solutions for the revival of trade with Brazil.

A week before receiving the minister's answers, the *Cortes* turned its attention to the appreciation of an autonomous opinion issued by the Public Finance Committee on the same subject, demonstrating the simultaneous commitment of the legislative power and the executive power in finding a suitable solution to the problem of the amortisation of paper money (*DC* 1821, 2606–08). The committee's opinion outlined the history of the issue and circulation of paper money, lamenting the State's failure to comply with its obligations and its consequent discredit. Although this opinion was centred almost exclusively on finding a financial solution, through the establishment of a national bank, it did not substantially differ from the answer that would be presented the next day by the minister José Inácio da Costa.[9]

The proposal made by the Treasury Minister was also discussed outside parliament, thus keeping alive the public controversy with allusions to the parliamentary debates and their echoes in the press, testifying to the people's wish to participate in a debate and anticipating solutions that would involve the creation of a bank destined to gather together the paper money in circulation and, in this way, limit the restrictions on the functioning of a sphere of monetary circulation that was essential for revitalising the productive and commercial economic fabric (*Considerações excitadas* 1821; Madre Deus 1821).

A fundamental question underlying most of the proposals and considerations made about this theme was the need for a rigorous calculation of the amount of paper money in circulation, which, in turn, would make it possible to identify the amount of the State's public debt. The estimates that appeared in the texts of that time display some differences. Diogo Ratton (1821) referred to a total of 12 million *réis*, showing that he had a precise notion of the amount in question.

The calculation that was made later by the newly created Board of Public Credit, which succeeded the Board of Interest of Royal Loans, took account of the issues and amortisations of paper money in the period before the installation of the *Cortes Constituintes* (Table 4.2). The total amount of paper money issued between 1797 and 1807 was roughly 17,000 *contos*, corresponding to approximately 30 per cent of the supply of money in circulation, a percentage value that would still be the same at the beginning of the 1820s, when there was a fall in the amount of specie in circulation in accordance with the fall in economic activity in the years preceding the liberal revolution (Valério 2006, 33–35).

According to the same source (*Coleção de contas* 1836, Mapa 3, F. nº14), the Board of Interest undertook the payment of the public debt interest, between 1800 and 1816, amounting to 3,550,500$446, which made it possible to soften the sometimes catastrophic tone used to criticise the State's total failure to meet its obligations and commitments towards its creditors.

Thus, in December 1821, when the details of the proposal for the creation of the Bank of Lisbon were discussed in Parliament, its members could not ignore the multiple contributions originating from an enlightened public sphere that was aware of the important opportunity that the political moment provided.

*Table 4.2* Issue and amortisation of paper money, 1797–1820 (in *réis*)

| | | |
|---|---|---|
| Issue between 1.08.1797 and 6.12.1799 | 16,513,720$000 | |
| Amortisation between 30.03.1798 and 26.11.1799 | | 5,820,243$000 |
| Issue between 28.06.1805 and 31.03.1806 | 499,994$400 | |
| Issue of 31.10.1807 | 163,118$400 | |
| Total in circulation (c. 1820) | 11,356,589$800 | |

Source: *Coleção de contas* 1836, 3–4; Pinto 1839, 21.

## 4.6 Parliamentary debates and the creation of the Bank of Lisbon

The debate that was held in the *Cortes Constituintes* about the proposal to create a national public bank (this was the original title), presented by the Public Finance Committee, was an intense one. This proposal reiterated the opinion of the same committee, which had been presented in a parliamentary session on 11 October, without ignoring the report of the Treasury Minister, which had been read in the session of 12 October, and 'examining the different memoranda that had been sent relating to the foundation of public banks linked to the amortisation of paper money'.[10] One of the most prominent of these proposals was certainly the one presented by the deputy Francisco Soares Franco, who had submitted his project on 30 July 1821.

The beginning of the debate took place at the session of 13 December 1821, with a speech by Francisco Soares Franco. The process was then considered to have been completed and the decree for the establishment of the Bank of Lisbon was approved at the parliamentary session held on 29 December 1821, with the publication of a legal charter on the last day of the year.

In the first appreciation of the project, as a whole, the deputies were almost unanimous in recognising the advantages and needs for the existence of a bank, both from the point of view of national interest and from the prospect of the profits or dividends that it might provide for its shareholders. The only dissenting voice was that of the deputy Luís Monteiro, who considered that the creation of the bank should only take place after the process for the redemption of paper money had been duly regularised. But it was precisely this motive that served as the main argument for the most enthusiastic defenders of the creation of the bank – namely Soares Franco, Ferreira de Moura, Xavier Monteiro and Ferreira Borges– or, in other words, it was precisely in order to resolve the question of paper money that the members of the Public Finance Committee thought it was urgent to approve the way in which such a bank would operate.

Besides this primary function, the project also outlined the intention that the bank could serve as a state creditor, through a loan that would enable the Exchequer or National Treasury to fulfil its obligations of redeeming and amortising the public debt. As far as this last point was concerned, there were;

however, some voices expressing their disagreement in relation to the possibility of the bank making such a loan in the first year of its establishment, in order to guard against the possible dangers of decapitalisation on the part of those investing in the bank's shares. The concern with the constitution of the bank's capital was also visible in these initial interventions, in which the wish was expressed for the creation of a programme of incentives and rewards to attract potential shareholders.

In relation to these and other subjects that might be a factor of division between the deputies, namely the rate of interest to be charged by the bank in its operations, Ferreira Borges displayed some pragmatism in considering that the most important thing was to create the bank, leaving the details about its functioning and administration until later.

Once the project had been formally accepted as a whole, the discussion then began of each of its articles. In the debate on article 1, relating to the title of the bank, approval was given to the name of the Bank of Lisbon, proposed by the deputy João Rodrigues de Brito, as this was considered to be the name that would best express the private nature of the bank. This therefore meant discarding the proposal of the Public Finance Committee (National Public Bank) and the suggestions of calling it the Bank of Portugal or the National Bank. It was also the same Rodrigues de Brito who questioned the reference in the bank's articles of association to the 'protection of the *Cortes*'. He felt that, within the context of the activities of the new institutions that were emerging through the will of private citizens, such a phrase could be interpreted as a form of favouritism running contrary to the idea of impartiality. But the doubt was resolved by Borges Carneiro, who reminded people of the parliament's mission in promoting public utility, of which the bank was a good example.

Articles 2–8 (relating to the bank's capital and its subscription, the functioning of the General Meeting and the annual election of its directors, the preparation of the regulations and the exclusive nature of the existence of one single bank for a period of 20 years) were approved with slight alterations in relation to the original proposal, but without any significant debate about its contents.

Article 9 was one of the articles that gave rise to the greatest debate. The controversy was around the regulation of the mortgaging of property given as a guarantee in the discounting of bills of exchange. Different arguments were produced in relation to this matter, coming from deputies who considered that such mortgages should cause the property to revert to the bank's shareholders, in the event of a failure on the part of private citizens to pay the bills of exchange; others thought that such a privilege would be excessive and that, consequently, the mortgages should be disputed in the courts that were set up for this purpose; while yet others preferred to punish situations of non-compliance with prison sentences. At the end of a long debate, the approved proposal was not far removed from the original text, with a certain attitude of prudence prevailing that the general laws relating to competitions or disputes over the bankruptcies of businessmen should be applied in such cases. At many different moments in the debate, the central question ceased to be the regulation of mortgages, and instead turned into the existence of privileges (in this case, of direct access to the ownership of seized assets, without the need for the realisation of public deeds), which became an attractive element for the process of subscribing the bank's capital.

Among the most relevant parliamentary interventions, attention was drawn to the pedagogical speeches proffered by José Ferreira Borges (about the nature and practice of mortgages) and Manuel Fernandes Tomás, about the principles of justice applied to the assessment of the privileges of creditors. This matter was a pretext for demanding a public register of mortgages, with a view to obtaining a broader knowledge, and so that these same mortgages could be negotiated by those who might be interested in them.

An identical debate took place in relation to the discussion of Articles 10 and 11, relating to the granting of loans on assets pledged as security, especially in relation to the constitution of mortgages on real property that the bank should demand as security for the loans that it made. Besides the legal question already dealt with in the discussion of the justice associated with the realisation of mortgages and the execution of seized assets, the debate showed itself to be particularly significant in the exchange of opinions about the question of knowing whether the bank should or should not act as a bank that would finance the capital to be used for investment in productive activities. The arguments in favour of the bank performing such a role did not prevail. But it is worth registering the opinion defended by the deputy Francisco de Lemos Bettencourt:

> As agriculture in Portugal is in a state of great decline, needing support and protection: nothing could be easier than for each individual to be able, in particular through the establishment of the bank, with some mortgage or surety, to have someone to supply them with what they most need so that their property has some value and can begin to have some vigour and solidity.
> (*DC* 1821, 3478)

An opposite opinion was voiced by the deputy and magistrate José Peixoto Sarmento de Queirós:

> Let us not confuse ideas: funds that are destined for agricultural companies and industrial establishments are very useful: but their nature must be very different from these: for this purpose, we already have the funds of the brotherhoods, confraternities and other corporations; others may be set up and the bank can be limited solely to circulation, which is its object, and which does not permit the transactions that it performs from lasting for longer than just a few months.
> (*DC* 1821, 3480)

In this way, the parliamentary debate about the creation of the Bank of Lisbon was also an opportunity to draw attention to the range of functions that a bank could be called upon to perform, or, to put it another way, the different types of bank that it could function as. In the discussion that was held in the *Cortes*, in December 1821, it was not yet opportune to legislate banking operations for the financing of productive economic activities.

Once this essential disagreement had been overcome, Articles 12–15 were approved without any debate or any significant disputes. These articles stipulated the main activities that the bank might dedicate itself to: the purchase and sale of paper money, deposits of private citizens in a current account (demand deposit) and a fixed-term deposit account (interest-bearing), remaining exempt from the payment to the State of any taxes or charges for such operations. There were also no disputes relating to the approval of articles 16 and 17, which established the operations that the bank was prevented from undertaking: insurance business, mercantile operations of buying and selling; and sales and investments in real property (beyond the purchase of its own premises).

One of the deputies and members of the Public Finance Committee that most stood out in the course of the debates was José Ferreira Borges, who sought to maintain a pedagogical posture and to display himself as a figure of authority, demonstrating his vast knowledge about European banking organisation and about the most crucial legal questions relating to bank operations. He was also one of the people who most frequently quoted the opinions of the main foreign political economists, in which he was accompanied, and even surpassed, by the deputy João Rodrigues de Brito. These two deputies both made well-grounded speeches about the discussion of Article 18, relating to the issue of banknotes. For this purpose, they gathered together references to the works of Smith, Say, Storch, Ganilh and Sismondi, in order to underline the care that needed to be taken in controlling the issue of banknotes. They both defended the idea that the banknotes that were issued should not represent a value of more than half of the specie in circulation, and considered that it would not be advisable to issue banknotes with a low value. In their arguments, they did not forget the teachings that were provided by the science of political economy, nor the importance of parliament as a privileged place for promoting 'the interaction of economic doctrine, political practice and the train of events' (Gordon 1976, 1). Or, in other words, demonstrating in practice the central role of the parliamentary debates for the creation of new economic and financial institutions.[11]

At various moments in the parliamentary debate about the bank's articles of association, the problem was raised of the autonomy of the bank's decisions and its independence in relation to the orders and guidelines issued by the government and the *Cortes*. This theme was particularly acutely debated in the discussion of Article 19, which was also related to the right to issue banknotes, with the deputies seeking to base their arguments on a fundamental political option: leaving the subject to the control of the law dictated by the *Cortes*, or to the discretionary decisions taken freely by the bank's directors. The same tension between the rules imposed by the laws of the kingdom and the discretionary autonomy of the bank's governance was noted in the discussion of Article 23, which dealt with the loan that the bank was forced to make to the National Treasury, in return for the prerogatives and privileges arising from its creation, as well as in the discussion of Article 30, which established the possibility of making new loans in the future.

## Notes

1 The estimate erred on the side of optimism. According to the values compiled by Jaime Reis, the value estimated for the income was correct, but the expected expenditure would be around 10,583 *contos*, in total, or, in other words, the public accounts would present a deficit of roughly 2,900 *contos* (Reis 1996, 37).
2 For the English case in relation to this same topic, see Capie 2004.
3 Regarding these various concepts of the public debt and its issue in Portugal, cf. Valério 2001, 109–110.
4 On the parliamentary debates on budgetary matters relating to the period considered here, cf. Bastien 2005, 13–27.
5 External loans would only be resorted to in the context of the civil war of 1832–34, creating added difficulties in sustaining the State's financing that would mark the history of the Portuguese constitutional monarchy throughout the nineteenth century. For an overview of the evolution of the internal and external public debt in the subsequent stages of the process for the construction of the liberal State, as well as for an examination of the solutions for financial recovery with implications for tax reform, cf. Cardoso and Lains 2010 and Esteves 2005.
6 Arquivo Histórico Parlamentar, *Comissão de Fazenda* (AHP, CF). A selection of these petitions and reports was published in Pinheiro 1991, whose approach highlights the characteristics of the petitionary movement and its implications for the reform of the *ancien régime's* tax system, as well as the problem of the accumulation of wages and pensions among public servants.
7 AHP, CF, secção I/II, Cx. 118, mç. 81, doc. 54.
8 The details of these operations and their respective interest were stated in Article XX of the Legal Charter of the Bank of Lisbon, whose English translation that is reproduced in the Appendix of this book.
9 On the subtle differences between these proposals, cf. Nunes 2018, 96–99.
10 The text that we use here is the original manuscript signed by the members of the Public Finance Committee, Francisco Xavier Monteiro, José Ferreira Borges, Francisco de Paula Travassos, Francisco Barroso Pereira and Manuel Alves do Rio (*Projeto de Banco Público Nacional* 1821).
11 On the role and uses of political economy at the *Cortes Constituintes* of 1821–22, cf. Cardoso 1991.

## References

Almeida, António José Pedroso de, 1822. *Discurso breve sobre o estado da administração da fazenda pública e meios de se conseguir a sua reforma*. Lisboa: Tipografia Rollandiana.

Anonymous, 1821. *Parecer enviado à Comissão de Fazenda* (manuscript). Arquivo Histórico Parlamentar, Cortes Constituintes 1821–1822, Comissão de Fazenda, secção I/II, Cx. 117, mç 80, doc. 28.

A.T.C.S., 1822. *Plano sobre a amortização do papel-moeda oferecido ao Soberano Congresso e remetido à respetiva Comissão por A.T.C.S. em 1821, e hoje publicado a favor da viúva do autor*. Lisboa: Tipografia Silviana.

Azevedo, Francisco Gomes Veloso de, 1822a. *Método de evitar a introdução do falso papel-moeda, e extinguir o que atualmente circula*. Lisboa: Tipografia Rollandiana.

Azevedo, Francisco Gomes Veloso de, 1822b. *Indicação de projeto sobre a amortização da dívida pública, oferecido à iluminada consideração do Soberano Congresso*. Lisboa: Tipografia Rollandiana.

Bastien, Carlos, 2005. Os debates orçamentais nos primórdios da monarquia constitucional. In: Nuno Valério (coord.), *Os Orçamentos no Parlamento Português*. Lisboa: Assembleia da República e Publicações Dom Quixote, 13–62.

Bordalo, José Joaquim, 1821. *Plano oferecido em benefício da pátria a sua Majestade Fidelíssima Senhor D. João VI no dia 5 de Dezembro de 1820*. Lisboa: Imprensa Morandiana.

Borges, José Ferreira, 1831. *Princípios de Sintelologia: compreendendo em geral a teoria do tributo, e em particular observações sobre a administração, e despesas de Portugal, em grande parte aplicáveis ao Brasil*. Londres: Impresso por Bingham.

Caetano, António Alves, 2006. Finanças Públicas Portuguesas antes da Revolução de 1820. *Revista do Tribunal de Contas*, n° 46, 637–695.

Caetano, António Alves, 2013. *"Os Socorros Pecuniários" Britânicos destinados ao Exército Português (1809–1814) – Subsídios para a História da Guerra de Libertação Nacional*. Lisboa: author's edition.

Capie, Forrest, 2004. Money and economic development in eighteenth-century England. In: Leandro Prados de la Escosura (ed.), *Exceptionalism and Industrialization. Britain and its European Rivals, 1688–1815*. Cambridge and New York: Cambridge University Press, 216–232.

Cardoso, José Luís, 1991. A legislação económica do vintismo: economia política e política económica nas Cortes Constituintes. *Análise Social*, n° 112/113, 26:3/4, 471–488.

Cardoso, José Luís and Lains, Pedro, 2010. Public finance in Portugal, 1796–1910. In: José Luís Cardoso and Pedro Lains (eds.), *Paying for the Liberal State. The Rise of Public Finance in Nineteenth-Century Europe*. Cambridge and New York: Cambridge University Press, 251–278.

*Carta Constitucional da Monarquia Portuguesa*, 1826. Lisboa: Impressão Régia.

Carvalho, José Liberato Freire de, 1822. Dívida pública, e rigorosa necessidade de estabelecer os meios de a pagar. *O Campeão Português em Lisboa ou o Amigo do Povo e do Rei Constitucional*, I:XI, 15 Junho, 161–176.

*Coleção de contas da comissão interina da Junta de Crédito Público até Setembro de 1836*, 1836. Lisboa: Imprensa Nacional.

*Considerações excitadas pela resposta do Exmo. Ministro da Fazenda aos dois quesitos que lhe fez o Soberano Congresso: qual é a causa do aumento do desconto do papel-moeda? Qual o remédio próprio de minorar, ou destruir este mal? E alguns reparos sobre duas censuras*, 1821. Lisboa: Tipografia Rollandiana.

*Considerações importantes sobre o papel-moeda, dívida pública, contrabandos, alfândegas, indústria, e comércio nacional, etc.*, 1821. Lisboa: Imprensa Nacional.

*Constituição Política da Monarquia Portuguesa*, 1822. Lisboa: Imprensa Nacional.

Costa, José Inácio da, 1821. Qual é a causa do aumento do desconto do papel-moeda? Qual é o remédio próprio de minorar, ou de destruir este mal? – Relatório do Ministro da Fazenda. In: *Diário das Cortes Gerais e Extraordinárias da Nação Portuguesa*, n° 198, sessão de 12 de outubro de 1821, 2618–2620.

Costa, Vicente José Ferreira Cardoso da, 1822. *Os bons desejos de um português, ou a sua receita para se animar a circulação paralisada, acudindo-se aos males do papel-moeda e à miséria pública* (. . .). Lisboa: Tipografia de António Rodrigues Galhardo.

[*DC*] *Diário das Cortes Gerais e Extraordinárias da Nação Portuguesa.;* and *Diário da Câmara dos Senhores Deputados da Nação Portuguesa*. Lisboa: Impressão Régia, 1821–1822; 1822–1823 and 1826–1828.

Epiménides, 1822. Urgência de estabelecer o crédito público. E como se pode ele estabelecer? *O Independente*, Suplemento ao n° 34, 12 de fevereiro 1822, 394–398.

Esteves, Rui Pedro, 2005. Finanças públicas. In: Pedro Lains and Álvaro Ferreira da Silva (eds.), *História Económica de Portugal, 1700–2000*. Lisboa: Imprensa de Ciências Sociais, Vol. 2, 305–335.

F.J.C.F., 1821. *Memória sobre o aumento do valor representativo das peças, ou meias dobras e aplicação do mesmo aumento para a amortização do papel-moeda*. Lisboa: Impressão de João Baptista Morando.

Franzini, Marino Miguel, 1827. *Ensaio sobre o orçamento da dívida pública, receita, e despesa do Tesouro do reino de Portugal no ano de 1826*. Lisboa: Impressão Régia.

Freire, José Joaquim, 1821. *Projeto de desconto e amortização do papel-moeda através da criação de um Banco* (manuscript). Arquivo Histórico Parlamentar, Cortes Constituintes 1821–1822, Comissão de Fazenda, Cx. 118, mç 81, doc. 51.

Gallard, Diogo Maria, 1821. *Memória sobra a utilidade e fáceis meios para estabelecer em Lisboa um Banco Nacional com caixa de desconto anexa do papel-moeda circulante* (manuscript). Arquivo Histórico Parlamentar, Cortes Constituintes 1821–1822, Comissão de Fazenda, Cx. 117, mç 80, doc. 25.

Gordon, Barry, 1976. *Political Economy in Parliament, 1819–1823*. London: Macmillan.

I.F.P.B., 1822. Projecto para pagar a dívida pública, sem para ela se desembolsar cousa alguma por espaço de cinco anos. *O Campeão Português em Lisboa ou o Amigo do Povo e do Rei Constitucional*, I:III, 33–35, 20 Abril 1822, and I:IV, 62–63, 27 Abril 1822.

Jordão, João Lineu, 1821. *Meio fácil natural, e proveitoso de sobreviver às fatais consequências do papel-moeda tornado e descrédito pelo estado infeliz das Finanças* (manuscript). Arquivo Histórico Parlamentar, Cortes Constituintes 1821–1822, Comissão de Fazenda, Cx. 117, mç 80, doc. 22.

Loureiro, João, 1821. *Projeto de Banco de Lisboa* (manuscript). Arquivo Histórico Parlamentar, Cortes Constituintes 1821–1822, Comissão de Comércio, Secção I/II, Cx. 67, doc. 68.

Madre Deus, Faustino José da, 1821. *Ensaio sobre o crédito e amortização do papel-moeda. Oferecido ao Soberano Congresso em 22 de outubro de 1821* (manuscrito). Arquivo Histórico Parlamentar, Cortes Constituintes 1821–1822, Comissão de Fazenda, Cx. 117, mç 80, doc. 5.

Medeiros, Filipe Arnaud de, 1820a. *Memória sobre a possibilidade e meios de pagar a dívida do Estado*. Lisboa: Impressão Régia, 1820.

Medeiros, Filipe Arnaud de, 1820b. Resposta à Refutação à Memória da amortização da dívida pública. *Mnemosine Constitucional*, nº 77 (22 Dezembro 1820), nº 78 (23 Dezembro 1820) e nº 79 (26 Dezembro 1820).

*Memória sobre o rebate do papel-moeda*, 1821. Lisboa: Tipografia Rollandiana.

Milheiro, João da Mata, 1821. *Reflexões e Plano para a extinção do ágio da moeda-papel e amortização da mesma moeda* (manuscript). Arquivo Histórico Parlamentar, Cortes Constituintes 1821–1822, Comissão de Fazenda, secção I/II, Cx. 118, mç. 81, doc. 39.

Moniz, José de Sousa, 1820. *Plano para se extinguir a dívida nacional tanto antiga como moderna, oferecido ao Supremo Governo do Reino*. Lisboa: Tipografia de Bulhões.

Moniz, Nuno Pato, 1822. Dívida pública. *Jornal da Sociedade Literária e Patriótica*, nº 1, 16 abril 1822, 41–47.

Moreira, Cristina, Reis, Jaime e Sousa, Rita, 2021. *Portugal's Napoleonic War: Cost, Loss, Missed Opportunity 1793–1851* (forthcoming).

Moura, José Joaquim Ferreira de, e Tomás, Manuel Fernandes, 1821. O Banco de Lisboa. *O Independente*, nº 20, 17 de dezembro de 1821.

Moura, José Joaquim Ferreira de, e Tomás, Manuel Fernandes, 1822. Aos capitalistas que recusam entrar no banco. *O Independente*, nº 29, 6 de fevereiro de 1822.

Nunes, João Andrade, 2018. Contributo para um estudo histórico-jurídico do Banco de Lisboa. *Revista de Direito das Sociedades*, IX:1, 79–133.

Pinheiro, Magda, 1991. *Os Portugueses e as Finanças no Dealbar do Liberalismo*. Lisboa: Edições João Sá da Costa.

Pinto, Agostinho Albano da Silveira, 1839. *Dívida Pública Portuguesa. Sua história, progresso e estado atual*. Lisboa: Imprensa Nacional.

Pinto, António Joaquim de Gouveia, 1820. *Memória em que se mostra a origem e progresso do papel-moeda em o nosso reino, e apontam os meios de verificar a sua amortização*. Lisboa: Impressão Régia.

*Projeto de Banco Público Nacional*, 1821. Arquivo Histórico Parlamentar, Secção VI, Cx 133, Mç 4-A, capa 26, doc 12.

*Projeto ou Memória sobre um novo sistema de organização do Erário ou Tesouro Nacional, com um método de escrituração análogo ao mesmo sistema*, 1821. Lisboa: Oficina de Simão Tadeu Ferreira.

Ratton, Diogo, 1821. *Reflexões sobre o papel-moeda em circulação. Em 11 de Outubro de 1821*. Lisboa: s/n.

*Refutação à Memória da amortização da dívida pública de Filipe Arnaud de Medeiros*, 1820. Lisboa: Impressão de Alcobia.

Reis, Jaime, 1996. *O Banco de Portugal. Das origens a 1914*. Lisboa: Banco de Portugal.

Ricci, José Ezequiel da Costa, 1820. *Plano para o estabelecimento da igualdade do giro da moeda papel, e sua insensível extinção, oferecido aos cidadãos portugueses, pela imparcialidade patriótica de . . . .* Lisboa: Impressão Régia.

Roma, Carlos Morato, 1822. [Economia política (Artigo comunicado)]. *Jornal da Sociedade Literária e Patriótica*, nº 15, 4 de junho 1822, 437–440.

Santos, Francisco António dos, 1821. Projeto para amortização da dívida pública. *Diário das Cortes Gerais, Extraordinárias e Constituintes da Nação Portuguesa*, sessão de 5 de março de 1821, 210–212.

Sena, Manuel Rodrigues Lucas de, 1821. *Papel-moeda fora. Oferece aos Ilustríssimos e Excelentíssimos Senhores Deputados das Cortes* (manuscript). Biblioteca Nacional de Portugal, Fundo Geral, HG 10629.

Sequeira, João Henriques, 1821. *Banco de Socorro ou Banco de empréstimo sobre penhores* (manuscript). Arquivo Histórico Parlamentar, Cortes Constituintes 1821–1822, Comissão de Fazenda, Secção I/II, Cx. 118, mç. 81, doc. 40.

Silveira, José Xavier Mouzinho, 1822. [Relato de debate sobre crédito público]. *Jornal da Sociedade Literária e Patriótica*, nº 26, 11 outubro 1822, 705–713.

Silveira, José Xavier Mouzinho da, 1826–1828. Notas sobre a situação das finanças. In: Mouzinho da Silveira, *Obras, Manuscritos e Impressos*. Lisboa: Fundação Calouste Gulbenkian, 1989 (edited by Miriam Halpern Pereira), Vol. II, 1095–1096.

Silveira, Luís Espinha, 1987. Aspetos da evolução das finanças públicas portuguesas nas primeiras décadas do século XIX (1800–1827). *Análise Social*, nº 97, 23:3, 505–529.

Tengarrinha, José, 1993. Venda dos bens da coroa em 1810–1820: os reflexos de uma crise nacional. *Análise Social*, XXVIII:122, 607–619.

Valério, Nuno, 2001. Os empréstimos do Estado. In: Nuno Valério (coord.), *As Finanças Públicas no Parlamento Português. Estudos Preliminares*. Lisboa: Assembleia da República e Edições Afrontamento, 109–209.

Valério, Nuno (ed.), 2006. *História do Sistema Bancário Português*. Lisboa: Banco de Portugal, Vol I.

Vam, João Carlos de, 1821. *Projeto para o estabelecimento de um banco nacional para o módico desconto do papel-moeda, e amortização dele assim como também das apólices grandes, e para uma companhia de seguradores terrestres, marítimo que forneçam meios aos lavradores precisados para continuarem as suas lavouras* (manuscript). Arquivo Histórico Parlamentar, Cortes Constituintes 1821–1822, Comissão de Fazenda, Cx. 117, mç 80, doc. 15.

# 5 The foundation and activity of the Bank of Lisbon

## 5.1 Statutory attributes and the mode of governance

The creation of the Bank of Lisbon was inseparable from a broadly shared concern for financial equilibrium, as was clearly expressed in the preamble to the Law that set it up,

> taking into account the public advantage resulting from the establishment of a Loan, Deposit and Discount Bank, which banishes usury, and promotes the convenience of transactions between individuals, and is simultaneously applicable to the amortisation of paper money.
>
> (*Regulamento* 1822, p. 3)[1]

In order that this aim of amortising the large amount of paper money in circulation could be realised, the Bank was legally obliged to lend the State the sum of 2,000 *contos* in banknotes, at an interest rate of 4 per cent, which would gradually replace the debt securities (*apólices*) that circulated as currency and whose uncontrolled issue had begun in 1796. The capital stock of the Bank of Lisbon was 5,000 *contos* (10,000 shares of 500,000 *reis* each, to be paid in equal parts of metallic and paper money) and its subscription would be made by individual shareholders, without any restrictions in terms of nationality, with the shareholders being able to sell or transfer the ownership of the shares and benefit from the half-yearly distribution of the dividends generated by the bank's activity. Consequently, it was a private bank with a public mission, established by the political will of the *Cortes*, which regarded the Bank of Lisbon as an instrument of credibility that would guarantee the proper functioning of the mechanisms of fiduciary circulation.[2]

The compulsory loan to the State had as its counterpart the benefits received by the Bank of Lisbon, namely those referring to the total exemption from taxes on banking operations and the State's obligation to accept banknotes issued by the bank in its public offices. The issuing of these banknotes enjoyed a monopoly of 20 years. The bank was thus protected against competition in the various profitable areas of business that it could be dedicated to, namely the discounting of bills of exchange, loans against pledges and mortgages, the

DOI: 10.4324/9781003355625-5

purchase and sale of public debt securities and gold and silver, deposits of specie and paper money and the collection of bills. It was, however, barred from undertaking business that involved risk and insurance, as well as trading in commodities and real estate.

As an institution, the Bank of Lisbon displayed similar characteristics to other private banks created in Europe at the same time, with its multiple purposes being linked by two primary functions serving the needs of the modern fiscal state: the amortisation and management of the public debt and the issuing of banknotes, in order to guarantee the efficiency of monetary circulation (Pohl 1994; Atack and Neal 2009). The Portuguese experience benefited greatly from the lessons provided by the trajectories of the Bank of England, created in 1694 (Temin and Voth 2013), the Bank of San Carlos, established in Spain in 1782 (Tedde de Lorca 1999) and the Bank of France, founded in 1800 (Bignon and Flandreau 2018). However, it clearly differentiated from other historical examples, given the process of its creation and the state protection granted by the legislative power.[3]

According to the bylaws, the management of the bank was entrusted to a board composed of a president and 16 directors, who would be of Portuguese nationality or naturalised as such, and would each own at least 12 shares in the bank. They would be elected annually by a General Meeting composed of the 150 principal shareholders. The number of elected directors and the number of members of the General Meeting were, in fact, to be changed in the first months following the beginning of the bank's activity (being fixed at eight directors and 100 members of the General Meeting), due to the scant and slow participation in the process of subscription to the bank's shares.

In fact, the difficulties in realising the capital of the Bank of Lisbon were promptly recognised and emphatically lamented by the Public Finance Committee at the *Cortes Constituintes*, less than a month after the promulgation of the legal charter:

> The Committee did not therefore expect that most of the Portuguese capitalists, some out of ignorance of their own interests, others due to some childish whim, and yet others, encouraged by the sordid profit to be made from the high rates for the discounting of paper money, and almost all of them professing a manifest disdain for the public cause, should declare themselves to be enemies of an establishment, to the existence of which the modern free nations owe the increase of their industry, and a great part of their independence.
>
> (*DC* 1821, 27–28)

The situation consequently required some regulatory flexibility in relation to the minimum conditions and practical rules to be established so that the Bank of Lisbon could begin its legally constituted operations.[4] Notwithstanding the initial obstacles and the reluctance of the business community to become fully involved, the statutory rules fixed by the bank's governance revealed signs of legal innovation in relation to the model for the functioning of a joint stock company and its deliberative bodies (Nunes 2018, 107–114).

The model for the governance of the Bank of Lisbon, established in the legal charter of its creation, provided for the involvement in its administrative acts of a General Meeting composed of the shareholders with the largest shares in the capital. Initially, the number of such members was fixed at the 150 largest shareholders, which was then reduced to 100 in February 1822, due to the low level of subscription to the bank's capital. The consultation of the minutes of the General Meetings between January 1822 and January 1828 (the period corresponding to the time span chosen for this study) allows us to form an understanding of the subjects that were dealt with at these shareholders' meetings. Due to the number and regularity of the meetings held each year (a total of 57 meetings were held in this period, or, in other words, an average of more than nine meetings per year), it can be concluded that this statutory body had an active and effective existence, with implications for the decision-making processes relating to the bank's fundamental activities.

The statutory obligation to annually elect the bank's board of directors (one president and eight directors), approve the report and accounts of the previous year and decide upon the distribution of dividends was always fulfilled at the beginning of January of each year. The General Meeting was also summoned to give its opinion on the resignation requests of some directors claiming that they were unable to render their services to the bank due to other professional business. It should be noted that, on various occasions, the General Meeting declined to accept such requests, in accordance with the principle that the holding of shares in the bank's capital and the choosing of shareholders were conditions and prerogatives that could not be passed over.

The General Meeting revealed some agility in finding operational solutions, overcoming what might be considered formal obstacles to the bank's regular functioning. Thus, in the first meetings held between March and June 1822, the General Meeting decided to fix the number of shareholders necessary for its constitution at 50, as well as not to accept votes by proxy, nor permit participation at its meetings of shareholders who, because of the small numbers of shares that they held, were not legally qualified to have the right either to attend or to vote. It was also at these first meetings, which preceded the formal opening of the bank's activity on 21 August 1822 that the General Meeting decided upon the location of the bank's premises and approved its internal regulations. The bank, which would be open to the public, would be installed in the building of the *Depósito Público* (Public Deposit) in Largo do Pelourinho, the present-day Praça do Município.

Also in the year 1822, decisions were taken about the face value of the banknotes to be issued by the Bank of Lisbon and about the opening of an agency for the discounting of the paper money in circulation, away from its own premises and operating outside the bank's normal opening hours. This activity would be subcontracted to a kind of consortium of brokers operating in the Lisbon market. In this way, the bank would extend its privileges to other agents with experience in the business. However, the most important decision of this initial year of 1822, and which was the subject of the most heated discussion, related to the opening of a loan to be granted to the government and its respective conditions. This matter, which had been latent since the phase of the parliamentary discussions, in December 1821, as the crucial and decisive question for the bank's creation, was approved, in general, at the sessions of the General Meeting of the Bank of Lisbon held on 16 and 23 September 1822. Despite this approval, there was a clear concern displayed by some shareholders in relation to the risk of decapitalisation caused by the large sum of money at stake, given that the paid-in capital in September 1822 amounted to 1,650 *contos*, while the value of the loan to be granted to the government was 1,200 *contos*, involving the payment of 5 per cent interest. As a guarantee of the loan, it was suggested at the General Meeting that the income from the tithe taxes should be mortgaged.

In 1823, the General Meeting held on 18 January decided to restrict consultation of its minutes and not to publish them in the press, which can be understood as an act of prudential management in relation to sensitive matters of a financial nature with implications for the administration of the system of public finances. An identical precaution was taken with the rejection of the proposal made by one director that the terms and conditions of the loan made by the bank to the government should be printed and made public. And it was in this same year that the General Meeting authorised the granting of loans against pledges, approved the bank's participation in the administration of the tobacco contract and requested the *Cortes* to introduce legislative measures that would enable the process for the redemption and extinction of paper money to be speeded up. This subject would be repeatedly brought up at General Meetings in subsequent years.

In 1824, the agenda of the 11 meetings held was almost exclusively dedicated to the discussion and approval of the bank's revised regulations at a politically sensitive time, which revealed how the Bank of Lisbon did not see either its existence or its functioning being affected by the political turning point of the absolutist uprising (*Vilafrancada)*. Although the minutes of the General Meeting do not offer any factual evidence about the political assent that would have been given by the bank's governing bodies, there is no doubt regarding the shared purposes between the government that emerged from the counter-revolutionary coup and the directors of the Bank of Lisbon, who, on 7 June 1824, received, with pomp and circumstance, and a famous figurative representation, the legal charter of rehabilitation granted by King João VI. Indeed, it would have been strange if it were not like this. In fact, it is worth remembering the obvious circumstance that the main and the most prominent shareholder of the Bank of Lisbon was Henrique Teixeira de Sampaio, the Baron of Teixeira and the 1st Count of Póvoa, who, in June 1823, after the *Vilafrancada*, began to perform the functions of Minister and Secretary of State for the Treasury, remaining in this position until January 1825. Or, in other words, the politician responsible for the financial administration of the kingdom was the largest shareholder of one of the State's main credit institutions, defying all the principles and purposes of autonomy and independence that the parliamentary discussions about the creation of the Bank of Lisbon had sought to safeguard. At the time, the matter was not considered susceptible to any political sensitivities, and, in this way, it enshrined a convergence between public service and private interest that seemed to be secured by the existence of mutual advantages.

The possibilities for growth in the bank's activities, thanks to the new political lease of life that it had been given, were demonstrated by the creation of a branch in Porto, whose regulations were discussed at various General Meetings of the bank held in the first months of 1825. The project of opening this branch had already been discussed in 1822, when the possibility was raised of delegating its representation to the *Companhia Geral de Agricultura e Vinhas do Alto Douro* (the General Company of Agriculture and Wine-Growing in the Alto Douro Region). However, the negotiations that were initiated between the Bank of Lisbon and the *Companhia* were not successful. The branch opened its doors on 16 March 1825, but ended up losing the justification to pursue such a low level of business, ceasing its activity at the beginning of 1828, and only being re-established in 1831.

At the General Meetings of the Bank of Lisbon in 1826 and 1827, there began to be a most evident concern on the part of the principal shareholders in relation to the government's pressures to make a new loan and to realise payments in advance through the bank to various public administration services, as well as about the cash-flow problems resulting from the demand for specie to be given in exchange for an increasing amount of discounted paper money. The suspension of transactions made with paper money and the opening of a new subscription of shares in order to increase the bank's capital were measures suggested in order to contain the crisis that seemed imminent and which would lead to the declaration to suspend the convertibility of banknotes and paper money into specie, whose significance will be discussed later on.

For the moment, what should be borne in mind is the dynamic participation of the shareholders of the Bank of Lisbon in the regularly held sessions of the General Meeting, imposing their vigilance and scrutiny of the acts of the directors that they themselves had elected.

## 5.2 Shareholders and directors

Earlier I mentioned and documented the difficulties encountered in the subscription of the bank's capital. Despite the legislative intention of endowing the bank with privileges and incentives for private agents, only a few of the great businessmen and capitalists were interested in investing significant sums in the constitution of the Bank of Lisbon. It was soon concluded that the initially planned capital of 5,000 *contos* would not be reached, so that this amount was reduced to half in August 1822, so as not to delay the beginning of the bank's entry into operation. Even so, it was only after the rehabilitation of the bank in 1824 that the total amount of its capital, fixed at 2,400 *contos* (4,800 shares of 500$000 *réis* each), was fully subscribed. In December 1827, a new increase in the bank's capital was decreed, with the issue of shares that would enable this sum to reach the amount of 5,000 *contos*. However, the amount that was subscribed was only 1,050 *contos*, thus increasing the capital to 3,450 *contos de réis*. The initial reference value of 5,000 *contos* would only be reached with a new capital subscription in 1834, in the aftermath of the Civil War (1832–34).

Through the general list of shareholders between 1822 and 1828, we can note the clear preponderance of one single shareholder, Henrique Teixeira de Sampaio, who, from July 1823, onwards bore the title of the first Count of Póvoa, which was given to him by King João VI as a reward for his participation in the *Vilafrancada* uprising. In the first year of the bank's activity, he had 400 shares, corresponding to 11.4 per cent of the bank's total subscribed capital. In 1828, he had 540 shares, a number that was higher than the sum total of shares owned by four businessmen who, between 1822 and 1828, each had more than 100 shares, namely: António Esteves Costa (160), Joaquim da Costa Bandeira, Baron of Porto Covo de Bandeira (112), Fernando Cardoso Maia (113) and José Bento de Araújo (110). One great businessman and capitalist who did not participate in the subscription of shares in the bank was Joaquim Pedro de Quintela, the first Count of Farrobo. However, the large and profitable business that he maintained in collaboration with both António Esteves Costa and the Baron of Porto Covo leads us to suppose that it was through these partners that he was able to exercise his presumable influence. Attention is also drawn to the presence in the list of shareholders of his sister and brother-in-law, the Countess and Count of Cunha, who held 60 shares in the first years of the bank's existence.[5]

The fundamental feature of the bank's shareholding structure is its highly scattered appearance (as can be seen in the following tables), due to the high total number of people holding at least one share, which was very close to the statutory limit of the number of shareholders with more than 12 shares in each year, or, in other words, with the right to participate in the General Meeting (with a limit of 100 members) and with the possibility of being elected to the bank's Board of Directors.

This subset of shareholders with more than 12 shares corresponded, on average, to roughly 23 per cent of the total number of shareholders (Table 5.1). Throughout the period considered here, the capital subscribed by this same subset represented, on average, roughly two-thirds of the bank's total capital (Table 5.2).

All the shareholders were either Portuguese or naturalised as such.[6] There are some women's names to be found in the list, who were certainly relatives or the heiresses of businessmen, representing roughly 6 per cent of the shareholders with more than 12 shares. Roughly 25 per cent of the shareholders with voting capacity were recorded in the lists of Lisbon businessmen whose names are to be found in the *Almanaques* published between 1812 and 1823.[7] They represented a new mercantile elite, the successors to the generation of businessmen who belonged to the networks responsible for the creation and reproduction

*Table 5.1* Number of shareholders, 1822–28

| | *1822* | *1823* | *1824* | *1825* | *1826* | *1827* | *1828* |
|---|---|---|---|---|---|---|---|
| > 12 shares | 93 | 96 | 120 | 124 | 121 | 123 | 175 |
| Total | 424 | 426 | 505 | 505 | 515 | 530 | 764 |

Source: AHBP, BL/001 *Registo Geral de Acionistas*

*Table 5.2* Concentration of capital, 1822–28 (in *contos*)

| | *1822* | *1823* | *1824* | *1825* | *1826* | *1827* | *1828* |
|---|---|---|---|---|---|---|---|
| Capital of shareholders > 12 shares | 1066<br>60.8% | 1104<br>63.0% | 1628.5<br>67.9% | 1634<br>68.0% | 1577.5<br>65.7% | 1646<br>68.6% | 2228.5<br>64.7% |
| Total capital | 1751 | 1751 | 2400 | 2400 | 2400 | 2400 | 3444 |

Source: AHBP, BL/001 *Registo Geral de Acionistas.*

of commercial and industrial wealth in the times of the Marquis of Pombal and Dom Rodrigo de Sousa Coutinho.[8] Many of them certainly prospered in the speculative business of redeeming paper money, trusting in the bank's capacity and guarantees to continue to develop this type of transaction. Others, perhaps the most powerful, benefited from the lucrative activities of supplying the Portuguese-British troops in the wars against the invading French army (as was the well-known case, for example, of Henrique Teixeira de Sampaio, Count of Póvoa).

Besides the mercantile and industrial agents, the fundamental body of shareholders of the Bank of Lisbon included jurists and magistrates, members of the recent aristocracy with links to the world of business, small property owners, liberal professionals and politicians with a seat in the *Cortes Constituintes* of 1821–22 (namely, António José Ferreira de Sousa, Francisco Xavier Monteiro, José Maria Xavier de Araújo, Luís Monteiro, Manuel Alves do Rio, Marino Miguel Franzini and Vicente António da Silva Correia), or who would later come to have a seat in the *Cortes* of 1826–28 (namely, Manuel Gonçalves Ferreira and José Joaquim Cordeiro).

The hard core of the directors of the Bank of Lisbon in the years considered here (1822 to 1828) was composed of the Baron of Porto Covo, António Esteves Costa and Fernando Cardoso Maia. These three influential businessmen certainly counted on the political backing of the Count of Póvoa, the principal shareholder, who never assumed any position in the leadership of the bank. In the first three years, they remained convergent in their stances under the leadership of the Baron of Porto Covo. However, between 1825 and 1827, the Baron of Porto Covo withdrew from power, leaving the running of the bank under the command of Esteves Costa and Cardoso Maia. Their unsuccessful management, which led to the bank's first crisis with the declaration of the

*Table 5.3* Deposits of private citizens, 1822–28 (in *réis*)

| *Year* | *Paper money* | *Metallic money* | *Total* |
|---|---|---|---|
| 1822 | 134,242$800 | 198,971$411 | 333,214$211 |
| 1823 | 502,626$000 | 515,361$575 | 1,017,987$575 |
| 1824 | 442,140$000 | 676,610$264 | 1,118,750$664 |
| 1825 | 418,815$600 | 658,701$041 | 1,077,516$641 |
| 1826 | 568,311$200 | 735,669$211 | 1,303,980$411 |
| 1827 | 470,059$600 | 644,645$689 | 1,114,705$289 |
| 1828 | 190,458$600 | 328,904$374 | 519,362$974 |

Source: Peres 1971, p. 519.

inconvertibility of banknotes and paper money in December 1827, dictated the return of the Baron of Porto Covo and his election as President in January 1828, a position that he continued to occupy until 1837.

The list of all the elected directors,[9] enables us to see that, in addition to the names mentioned, other shareholders regularly called upon to perform managerial functions included the businessmen Manuel Ribeiro Guimarães and Silvério Taibner, and the magistrate and deputy Manuel Alves do Rio. The participation of these and other businessmen and magistrates was certainly not due to the salaries that they received for exercising these managerial duties.[10] It was a responsibility and a statutory obligation that did; however, guarantee effective control of the operations to which the bank was dedicated.

The trust and confidence that the Bank of Lisbon inspired among the public can be assessed by the volume and diversity of the depositors that it succeeded in attracting. Besides the high value of the deposits of the Royal Exchequer or Public Treasury, which corresponded to the revenues deposited as a guarantee for the loan granted by the Bank of Lisbon, to the temporary safekeeping of cash existing at government offices and to the reimbursements of advance payments, we should also note the deposits made by countless foreign traders operating in the Portuguese markets and the deposits of the shareholders themselves (most notably the Count of Póvoa) and the bank's directors.[11] Thus, the liquidity that was needed for the operations to which the bank was dedicated was supported by a stable financial cushion that only showed signs of collapse towards the end of 1827, due to a conjunction of circumstances that I shall try to explain later on. Table 5.3 presents the evolution of the total amount of deposits of private citizens between 1822 and 1828.

## 5.3 Indicators of banking vitality (1822–1827)

The main political events that took place during this period – the *Vilafrancada* uprising, the conferral of the Constitutional Charter and Dom Miguel's attempts to usurp power – do not seem to have disturbed the climate of trust that the Bank of Lisbon had inspired among the economic and financial agents, both individual and collective, public and private, who were already benefiting from its operations. The Bank of Lisbon performed well in the aftermath of the absolutist counterrevolution, also withstanding the political changes that were subsequently introduced. The revocation of the Constitution of 1822 and all the liberal legislation produced since the beginning of the 1820 revolution had no effect on the situation of the Bank of Lisbon, which, curiously, was the only institution created by the liberal regime to keep its status unchanged, as well as seeing its legal existence reaffirmed and reinforced. The operating results of the Bank of Lisbon and the dividends distributed to the shareholders allow us to conclude that the contemporary political vicissitudes did not affect the bank's overall performance in the first six years of its existence, from its foundation until the crisis declared in December 1827[12].

The activity of the Bank of Lisbon over these years was described in great detail by Damião Peres, who closely followed the annual reports of the bank's management, which he then transcribed and included as an annex to his thoroughly researched heuristic study (Peres 1971). This is a most valuable secondary source, constructed from the original documentation kept in the Bank of Portugal's Historical Archive, and which has been used as the starting point for various interpretive works with a greater analytical scope (especially Reis 1996, but also Valério 2006 and Neves 2013). These studies make it possible to paint a portrait of the evolution of the main indicators of the activity of the Bank of Lisbon, which are retrieved and completed in the following tables.

Table 5.4 shows a sustainable relationship between the bank's equity and assets, especially in the years before the convertibility crisis of December 1827, which would be overcome with a new subscription of capital that enabled the bank to preserve the stability of its business.

The profitable nature of the Bank of Lisbon's operations is shown in Table 5.5. The trend towards an increase in the bank's profits was accompanied by an equally regular growth in the dividends paid per share, with a high yield

*Table 5.4* Equity and assets, 1823–34

| *Year* | *No. of subscribed shares* | *Equity (in contos)* | *Assets (in contos)* |
|---|---|---|---|
| 1823 | 3,502 | 1,751 | 6,746 |
| 1824 | 4,800 | 2,400 | 7,636 |
| 1825 | 4,800 | 2,400 | 10,491 |
| 1826 | 4,800 | 2,400 | 10,421 |
| 1827 | 4,800 | 2,400 | 11,636 |
| 1828 | 6,888 | 3,444 | 9,665 |
| 1829 | 6,896 | 3,448 | 9,558 |
| 1830 | 6,904 | 3,452 | 9,589 |
| 1831 | 6,912 | 3,456 | 9,415 |
| 1832 | 6,912 | 3,456 | 9,120 |
| 1833 | 6,912 | 3,456 | 9,518 |
| 1834 | 10,000 | 5,000 | 12,699 |

Source: Reis 1996, based on the *Livros dos Balanços* (Balance Sheets) of the Bank of Lisbon, nos. 1 to 3.

*Table 5.5* Profits and dividends, 1823–34

| *Year* | *Net profits (contos)* | *Profits with the State (contos)* | *Dividends per share (réis)* | *Yield (%)* |
|---|---|---|---|---|
| 1823 | 113.3 | 98.9 | 35$050 | 7.0 |
| 1824 | 207.8 | 154.1 | 43$200 | 8.6 |
| 1825 | 249.0 | 191.8 | 52$138 | 10.4 |
| 1826 | 273.4 | 247.5 | 50$000 | 10.0 |
| 1827 | 330.3 | 252.3 | 68$819 | 13.8 |
| 1828 | 118.8 | 108.8 | 17$246 | 3.4 |
| 1829 | 216.9 | 109.6 | 31$456 | 6.2 |
| 1830 | 214.9 | 111.5 | 31$086 | 6.2 |
| 1831 | 203.1 | 91.6 | 29$300 | 5.9 |
| 1832 | 179.8 | 185.6 | 26$000 | 5.2 |
| 1833 | 222.1 | 180.5 | 31$000 | 6.2 |
| 1834 | 582.8 | 337.1 | 40$500 | 8.1 |

Source: Peres 1971 and Reis 1996, based on the annual reports of the Management of the Bank of Lisbon.

that fell sharply with the crisis of 1827–28. This same table also enables us to see that the main source of profit from the bank's operations was the services that it rendered to the State.

In fact, between the years 1823 and 1828, the profits from such operations – namely, the interest from direct loans, the anticipation of future tax revenue, advance payments to civil servants – represented an average value of 82.7 per cent in relation to the total amount of the net profit obtained by the bank. As Jaime Reis neatly summed it up:

> Although it was not the official banker of the State, it would, however, be no exaggeration to state that, informally, throughout its career, the Bank of Lisbon was little more than the bank of the Portuguese State, having consistently been not only its largest client, but also its main activity and source of income.
>
> (Reis 1996, 98)

This statement is, above all, applicable to the first phase of activity of the Bank of Lisbon, between 1822 and 1827, during which it fulfilled its lending function through the loans recorded as shown in Table 5.6. The business objective of maximising the profits obtained and the dividends to be distributed to the shareholders justified the option of the directors of the Bank of Lisbon to boost its operations with the State, which were subject to less unpredictability and consequently only a limited risk. Thus, they administered the advantages of a privilege that derived precisely from the fulfilment of that public mission.[13]

However, the crucial question that had lain behind the creation of the Bank of Lisbon, or, in other words, the extinction of the paper money originating from the first loans at the end of the eighteenth century, still remained largely

*Table 5.6* Loans to the State, 1822–27

| *Legal framework* | *Objective* | *Amount (contos)* | *Interest rate (%)* |
|---|---|---|---|
| Law 31.12.1821 | Redemption of paper money | 2000 | 4 |
| Law 24.02.1822 | Amortisation of debt securities | 545 | 4 |
| Decree 25.091823 | State expenditure | 2000 | 5 |
| Charter 7.01.1826 | State expenditure | 1000 | 3 |
| Law 31.03.1827 | State expenditure | 2400 | 5 |

Source: Valério 2006.

unsolved. From the approximate total of 11,300 *contos* of paper money in circulation (see Table 4.2) only 2,900 *contos* were redeemed by the bank (Reis 1996, 96). Thus, the notes issued by the bank and that were already in circulation, estimated to amount to roughly 2,000 *contos*, did not imply the extinction of the paper money that the banknotes were supposedly intended to replace. The disturbances in the form of fiduciary circulation remained as an obstacle to the fulfilment of aims that had been explicitly and widely discussed during the preparatory phase of the creation of the Bank of Lisbon.

## 5.4 Signs of crisis

The central motivation that had presided over the foundation of the Bank of Lisbon continued to be one of the main concerns of politicians, business agents, political journalists, and the various actors in the public sphere, for whom the process of extinction of paper money could not be allowed to peter out, despite the slowness of its progress in the first years of the bank's existence.

It was this concern that was transmitted in the testimony of Cláudio Adriano da Costa (the son of the Minister of the Treasury during the *vintismo* period, José Inácio da Costa), the author of one of the best grounded texts written about this theme, both from the point of view of the knowledge that it displayed about similar historical experiences in other European countries (England, France and Spain) and from the point of view of the theoretical approach made by the main political economists of the period (Jacques Necker, James Steuart, Adam Smith, Jean-Baptiste Say and David Ricardo, among others). In his own words:

> Fortunately, we have arrived at a time when there is no government so odious that it directly wishes to make more issues of paper money in order to represent wealth, when it has nothing other than debts. Public opinion, that huge colossus that arouses so many fears and causes such disturbances to everything, and which nothing can resist, no longer agrees to the continuation of any government without credit.
>
> (Costa 1826, 12)

The letter that Cláudio Adriano da Costa addressed to the Minister of the Treasury (Hermano José Braamcamp, Baron of Sobral) was one of the first texts to be published, heralding a remarkable career as a publicist, a private business agent in the area of finance and insurance and a member of various committees and public institutions designed to promote economic improvements. In this text from his youth, he showed himself to be particularly alert to the failure of the French experience of issuing paper money (*assignats*) after the Revolution, gathering together various favourable statements made by figures of authority from the economic and financial thought of that time. The main attraction of this text of his (written in a style that was not always marked by any great literary quality) perhaps lay in the dialogue that it maintained with particularly relevant texts for the understanding of the options of monetary policy, most notably David Ricardo's writings about the convertibility of the paper money in circulation.

His plan for the extinction of paper money would require the collaboration and active participation of the Bank of Lisbon, in terms that could be summarised as follows: the Bank of Lisbon would collect all the paper money in circulation, giving in exchange the banknotes that it would itself issue; in return, the government would offer the bank as a guarantee a loan to the amount of half of the paper money collected, also paying an interest of 2.5 per cent on the total of the paper money that had been collected and promptly burned; the government would then inform the *Cortes* about the pace of the replacements of the securities (*apólices*) by banknotes so that it could decree the amortisation of what might remain as a surplus. Cláudio Adriano da Costa included in his project a table for the calculation of the interest and surpluses created by this operation, as well as an algebraic model that would enable him to estimate the time needed to complete the process for the redemption of paper money.

Regardless of the validity or pertinence of the calculations that he made, Cláudio Adriano da Costa's project had the enormous merit of alerting people to the risk of a banking crisis provoked by the excess of paper money in circulation. The reality of the situation would soon prove him right.

In fact, at the end of 1827, a critical situation of some importance was declared, which led the Bank of Lisbon's management to suspend the conversion of paper money and banknotes into specie). This decision was made public on 6 December in the following terms:

> The Directors of the Bank of Lisbon inform the public that the unexpected outflow of silver in exchange for its notes to be exported abroad has increased to the point where it has completely run out of all the silver that it possessed. It consequently now finds itself in the painful situation of not being able to continue exchanging its notes as promptly as it has been doing until now. It also wishes to state that the Board of Directors has officially notified the government, asking for precautionary measures to be taken; and, for its own part, the Board of Directors will mobilise all of its resources, in order that it may, as soon as possible, recommence the payment of its notes.
>
> (In *Retrospecto* 1850, 14–15)

The government reacted promptly through the publication of two ordinances on 10 December, in which it expressed its surprise and criticism regarding the situation that had been created and called upon the Bank of Lisbon to re-establish its commitments to the public:

> The Princess Regent, in the name of the King, very severely reprimands the same Board of Directors for its thoughtlessness, or rather the bad faith, with which it has sought to lay the blame on the government for this odious situation, declaring that the responsibility must be attributed solely to the same Board of Directors for the ineptitude with which it has conducted its mercantile operations in recent times and especially in these last few ill-fated days. (. . .)
>
> She also informs the same Board of Directors that, regardless of the fact that it does not fall within the attributions of the executive power, such a measure could never merit her royal approval, even when she has been informed of the real and effective state of the bank's current funds. And, furthermore, she declares that she hopes that the same Board of Directors will take the necessary measures to ensure that, within the shortest possible space of time, it will succeed in re-establishing the regularity of its payments, as is its obligation and as it is in its immediate interest to do so, whatever sacrifices it may have to make to achieve such a fair, honest and useful end.
>
> (In *Retrospecto* 1850, 15)

This positioning clearly demonstrated the attention given by the government to the activities of the Bank of Lisbon, whose solvency and credibility were fundamental for ensuring the stability of the financial system. In fact, the government's dependence on borrowing from the Bank of Lisbon to sustain the public debt, as well as the advances made on regular payments to the different sectors of public administration, justified the political warning concerning the breach of statutory obligations. The tone of the reprimand left no room for any doubts as to its interpretation. The supposed independence and autonomy of the bank's management and leadership were put to the test in a most vehement fashion, given the necessity for decisions to be taken that would satisfy the government's wishes.

The solutions desired by the bank's management for the problem caused by the crisis in the flow of metallic money, which would necessarily dictate the suspension of convertibility, consisted of four types of measures: the issue of bond certificates as a way of reimbursing the private citizens who were unable to convert their securities (*apólices*) or banknotes into specie, the sale of public debt securities and an increase in the bank's capital to five thousand *contos* (Valério 2006, 58–59). However, the difficulties of the economic and political conjuncture did not permit the fulfilment of such proposals and targets. The increase in capital was reduced to the amount of 3,450 *contos*, and the bank was forced to reduce the notes in circulation (passing from 2 thousand *contos* to roughly 400), and the deposits of private individuals fell to roughly half their previous amount (see Table 5.5). In view of this difficult situation in which the bank found itself, it was the bank's directors who gave their own personal guarantees or acted as creditors, in order to prevent the crisis worsening even further.[14]

## 5.5 Theoretical framework of the banking crisis

This context of a banking crisis served as an opportune pretext for the analysis and debate that José Ferreira Borges, one of the most important liberal politicians, produced on the subject (Borges 1827). It was therefore a time when the authors who were most fully versed in matters relating to monetary theory and policy could present arguments and proposals for overcoming the crisis affecting the Bank of Lisbon and its relationship with the public powers. Having recently arrived from his exile in London, after emigrating there in 1823 following the *Vilafrancada* uprising, the man who had been one of the *vintista* deputies most committed to the creation of the Bank of Lisbon took advantage of the occasion to criticise the path that the bank's directors had followed.

For Ferreira Borges, the explanation for the crisis declared by the Bank of Lisbon was not the one presented by the bank's directors, who claimed that the unfavourable balance of trade required payments abroad in bullion, thus giving rise to a run on the Bank by traders who needed this money to carry out their transactions. This excess demand for liquidity in bullion would have given rise to cash-flow difficulties, which, in turn, would have provoked fear and panic from holders of paper money, who suddenly demanded its conversion into specie.

Irrespective of whether these situations might have occurred, Ferreira Borges diminished their significance, on the one hand by explaining that commercial crises could not be treated like simple short-term episodes, and on the other hand, by demonstrating his knowledge of the automatic mechanisms of regulation between specie flows, price determination and the balance of trade. For those who were frightened by the outflow of money, he offered the explanation that this short-term effect would generate an increase in future competitiveness due to the reduction in domestic prices that would make export products more attractive. This was an abstract and theoretical explanation, undoubtedly based on the doctrinal conviction that 'nothing will better prove what can be attained from the absolute freedom of trade, than the study of our situation without it compared to the one we have already had with it' (Borges 1827, 28).

As far as the display of panic was concerned, Ferreira Borges considered it momentary and insignificant, compared to banking crises in other countries. In his opinion, the craving for bullion concealed the main reason for the suspension of convertibility that the bank's directors had approved, namely the excess of banknotes in circulation. In his words:

> The point of the Bank, therefore, was not due to any cause other than the *imprudent excessive* issue of its notes; because all the other causes, which influence the fall of similar establishments, have not been observed among

> us; and this to which the directors gave cause, had no influence whatsoever in such an event. There remains, therefore, only one, the excessive issue of notes; and it is evidently sufficient to produce such a result.
>
> (Borges 1827, 32)

Ferreira Borges was careful to explain that the issue of banknotes by the Bank of Lisbon had been fully justified by the need to withdraw and replace the paper money (initially equivalent to public debt securities) in circulation. And he was concerned about explaining that the evil lay not in the issue of banknotes, which were a fundamental resource for guaranteeing monetary circulation, but rather in the excess amount that was issued.

One of the appeals of this text by Ferreira Borges is the way in which he developed his argument by comparing the situation experienced by the Bank of Lisbon to the examples given by recent European banking history, namely the Bank of England and the Bank of France. Recalling that the institutional nature of the Bank of Lisbon was similar to that of the Bank of England (a private bank engaged in circulation and deposit activities, but also fulfilling the role of state lender and the agency administering the public debt), Ferreira Borges relied on the Bank of England's experience to show that the magnitude of the situation which led to the suspension of the convertibility of its notes in 1797 was not comparable to the episode which afflicted the directors of the Bank of Lisbon in 1827. Ferreira Borges was implicitly assuming that the Bank of Lisbon's scant experience was not comparable to the lasting reputation that the Bank of England had established.[15] In fact, the credibility and public trust that the Bank of England enjoyed was sufficient reason for the economic agents not to fear any long-term consequences from its decision to interrupt the convertibility of the banknotes into specie.[16]

In addition to the historical evidence, Ferreira Borges also relied on the theoretical arguments provided by political economists attentive to monetary phenomena and banking crises, such as Heinrich Storch, Thomas Joplin, David Buchanan, John R. McCulloch and, above all, the 'wise economist and financier David Ricardo' (Borges 1827, 16). Knowing Ricardo's scepticism about the role of the banks in ensuring money market equilibrium, as well as his favourable opinion about the existence of a single issuing bank, Ferreira Borges explicitly cited the text by Ricardo (1816) which more clearly underlined the adherence to a system of currency circulation based on flexibility and limited convertibility (not forced, but subject to the rules of the market) of banknotes into specie, that is, a system in which the invariability of the value of money prevails, through market equilibrium between money supply and demand, subject to monitoring and control procedures.[17] In this particular detail, Ferreira Borges followed Ricardo's broad vision of a money market that is not self-regulated and requires the assistance and control of a single (central) bank with a monopoly over the issue of banknotes.[18]

It is also worth noting how Ferreira Borges condemned the lack of transparency and reliable information provided by the Bank of Lisbon about its operations, calling for the need for public scrutiny to which the bank's activities necessarily had to be subject:

> Without this publicity, the bank's credit will always be more subject to the shocks inherent in similar institutions than if their frank and open march presents the public with its regularity. It is a great mistake to suppose that in this case the mystery is the foundation of its existence.
>
> (Borges 1827, 14)

José Ferreira Borges' text was not very favourably received by the bank's directors, who felt the need to reimpose their version of events by publishing a *Breve Ensaio* (Brief Essay, 1828), which was effectively an immediate reply to Ferreira Borges' interpretation of the banking crisis.

Although it was published without the identification of any individual author, this manifesto was the direct responsibility of the directors of the Bank of Lisbon. After recalling the bank's founding moments and first operations, it highlighted the service that it had provided to the government – through the discounting of paper money, the advances made on future revenue, the immediate and direct loans and the indirect loans made to the State's various offices and bodies – which clearly demonstrated the prevailing institutional collaboration and complicity, as was explicitly underlined:

> Through this brief exposition of the facts, evidence is provided of the cooperation that the government has always encountered at the bank, in order to help with its payments, and sometimes in the most difficult circumstances, as has been most clear.
>
> (*Breve Ensaio* 1828, 10)

In order to reassure the public and respond to the challenge of submitting the report about the state of the bank for general scrutiny, it presented a table showing the bank's stocks in bullion and paper money, corresponding to each of the bank's operations (ibid., 14–15) and making it possible to conclude that 'the solidity of the bank is evident, as is the security of all those to whom it has obligations' (ibid., 10).

The essence of the argument presented was centred on demonstrating that Ferreira Borges was wrong in considering that there was an excess of banknotes in circulation. The directors wrote, with a hint of irony, that

> it will not appear to anyone that this amount in circulation is exorbitant, excessive, and disproportionate to its capital. In view of the nature of the effects and securities that it holds, neither Jean-Baptiste Say, nor Storch would accuse the bank's directors of being less circumspect, or excessive in the issue of its banknotes.
>
> (ibid., 16)

Choosing the same field of theoretical knowledge in which Ferreira Borges had situated himself, they stated that the amount of banknotes in circulation (roughly 2,100 *contos*) was perfectly compatible with the proportion that the political economists recommended in such cases, or, in other words, that the issue of banknotes could reach as high as twice the bank's capital. In this case, as the bank's capital was 2,400 *contos*, the margin of issue was far from reaching the maximum acceptable limit.

Thus, for the directors of the Bank of Lisbon, the explanation that they had previously given about the excess demand for specie still remained valid, and they subtly added to this the undertakings that the bank had made to the State, withdrawing liquidity for the operations of converting paper money and banknotes into specie.

In order to justify their interpretation, they resorted (just like Ferreira Borges) to the history of the Bank of England, inserting a long excerpt from the translation published in 1801 of the book by Thomas Fortune about the history of this institution (Fortune 1801). The part of the book that was reproduced (pp. 21–57) made it possible to illustrate decisions taken by the bank of England in February 1797 (suspension of the conversion of banknotes into specie) which had served as inspiration for what the Bank of Lisbon had done in December 1827.

And so that there would be no doubts regarding the motivations for this text designed to redress the balance, the directors of the Bank of Lisbon provided the following clarification at the end of an additional note addressed especially to José Ferreira Borges (pp. 58–63):

> Finally: anyone who reads the publication by Mr José Ferreira Borges, must surely agree with us, as we said at the beginning of this supplementary note, that its author has developed great knowledge, and is endowed with great talent, having been able to appropriate the opinions of various authors; yet there are also in the same production some contradictions, and some shortages of information, perhaps arising from the short time that he had to compose his text, mainly with regard to the Bank of Lisbon, about which this present pamphlet may serve as a valuable addition.
>
> (*Breve Ensaio* 1828, 63)

The controversy that arose between José Ferreira Borges and the directors of the Bank of Lisbon demonstrates the commitment of the Portuguese political and financial elite in clarifying the public opinion about matters that, at the theoretical level, were certainly not within the reach of everyone; but which, at the level of their practical consequences, had implications in the everyday economic and financial life of the country, since what was at stake was the way in which the circulation of money could be turned into a more efficient process for all the agents involved in the systems of production and consumption.[19]

## Notes

1 The history of the Bank of Lisbon has merited the attention of various scholars, especially from the point of view of the study of the antecedents of the Bank of Portugal, established in 1846 after the merger between the Bank of Lisbon and the finance company *Companhia Confiança Nacional*. Cf. Amzalak 1919, Matta 1932–1933, Macedo 1963, Peres 1971, Soares 1971, Valério 2006, Neves 2013 and Nunes 2018. As already emphasised in Chapter 1 of this book, particularly worthy of attention is the contribution made by Reis 1996, who analysed the objectives and activities of the Bank of Lisbon in the light of the evolution of the Portuguese financial panorama of the first half of the nineteenth century (especially pp. 71–119).

2 This chapter is largely based on research of original sources concerning the activities of the Bank of Lisbon, kept at the Historical Archive of the Bank of Portugal, namely: lists of shareholders, list of directors and proceedings of General Meetings. The reader will find at the end of this chapter a list of the main collections relevant for this study [Sources].

3 On this issue and other peculiarities of the legal charter of the Bank of Lisbon, see Nunes 2018, 100–105.

4 Cf. *Regulamento* 1822, 14–24, which includes legislation and administrative acts relating to the process and time limit for subscribing to shares and the election of the Board of Directors of the Bank of Lisbon. The final version of the bank's regulations (ibid., pp. 27–51), published on 25 June, 1822, expresses the implementation of the legal charter that set up the Bank of Lisbon with the adaptations arising from the first phase of its creation.

5 On the financial investments of the Count of Farrobo in the initial phase of his colourful career as an entrepreneur, capitalist and financier, see Caetano 2020, 27–76.

6 It is beyond the scope of this study to make a detailed analysis of the shareholders' profiles. Some studies that have been made of other banking institutions, albeit for periods that do not coincide with this one, highlight the importance of such an approach, namely Robledo 1988, Reis 2010 and Aidar 2018.

7 I wish to thank Jorge Miguel Pedreira for providing me with information about these lists of businessmen.

8 On this subject, see Pedreira 1995. Although this study continues to be available only in the mimeographed version of his PhD dissertation, it still remains as a primary source that is indispensable for our knowledge of the Portuguese mercantile elite in the period under consideration.

9 Source: AHBP, BL/001 *Registo Geral de Acionistas*

10 Under the terms of the bylaws, the President's annual salary was 800$000 *réis*, while the directors received 600$000.

11 Source: *AHBP*, BL/020 – *Contas correntes de depósitos particulares* (1822–46)

12 According to Jaime Reis' division of this time into periods, this period of expansion was followed by a phase of economic contraction between 1828 and 1834 (or, in other words, during the Miguelist period and the Civil War), and then, once again by a period of expansion and consolidation until the merger between the Bank of Lisbon and the *Companhia Confiança Nacional* in 1846, giving rise to the Bank of Portugal (Reis 1996, 88–89).

13 It is worth noting that, in 1823, the Portuguese government began to seek external loans with the same purpose of securing payments and redeeming the public debt. The details of the first external loan contract, signed in September 1823 by the Portuguese Minister of Finance (at the time Henrique Teixeira de Sampaio, the Count of Póvoa, the main shareholder of the Bank of Lisbon) and the banking house of B.A. Goldschmidt, are described in Flandreau 2021.

14 See Peres 1971, 125–152, for a detailed account of the sessions of the bank's General Meeting and the measures that were put in place in combination with the government.

15 On the explanation of the restrictive policy pursued by the Bank of England following the decision of the non-convertibility of paper money in 1797, see Fetter and Gregory 1973 and Neal 1990, 180–181.

16 On the institutional reputation of the Bank of England in the context of the restrictive policy regarding the question of convertibility, see O'Brien and Palma 2020.

17 On Ricardo's ideas on money and banks, cf. Rosselli 1999, Arnon 2011, Deleplace 2013 and Diatkine 2013. For an overall view of banking activity in England in the period that Ferreira Borges took into consideration, see White 1984. For an overall appreciation of monetary and banking theories and policies in the classical school of political economy, see O'Brien 2004, Chapter 6.

18 It should be noted that Ferreira Borges was neither the first nor the only Portuguese author to quote this text from Ricardo. Cláudio Adriano da Costa (1826) had already done so the year before, in the text that I mentioned earlier.

19 The opposing views on the management of the Bank of Lisbon reveal some analogy with debates in England concerning the dispute between the Currency School and the Banking School. For an overview of this dispute, see Arnon 2011, Chapters 11 and 12.

## Sources

*(AHBP) Arquivo Histórico do Banco de Portugal* (Historical Archives of the Bank of Portugal)

BL/001 – *Registo geral dos acionistas* (1822–1846) – (List of shareholders)

BL/003 – *Índice de acionistas* – (Index of shareholders)

BL/004 – *Registo de títulos de ações* – (Registration of shares' owners)

BL/019 – *Índice dos livros de registo de contas correntes de depósitos particulares* – (Index of current accounts)

BL/020 – *Contas correntes de depósitos particulares* (1822–1846) – (Currrent accounts and private deposits)

BL/024 – *Acórdãos da Direção* (1822–1846) – (Decisons of the Board of Directors)

BL/030 – *Registo de papéis oficiais* (1821–1846) – (Registration of official papers)

PT/TT/BL – *Livros de Atas da Assembleia Geral do Banco de Lisboa* (1822–1846) – (Proceedings of the General Assembly)

## References


Aidar, Bruno, 2018. Financiar o império: o Banco do Brasil e seus acionistas, 1808–1821. *Working Paper, Instituto Mora*. México.

Amzalak, Moses A., 1919. *O Banco de Lisboa*. Lisboa: Instituto Superior de Comércio de Lisboa.

Arnon, Arie, 2011. *Monetary Theory and Policy from Hume and Smith to Wicksell. Money, Credit and the Economy*. Cambridge and New York: Cambridge University Press.

Atack, Jeremy and Neal, Larry (eds.), 2009. *The Origin and Development of Financial Markets and Institutions. From the Seventeenth Century to the Present*. Cambridge and New York: Cambridge University Press.

Bignon, Vincent and Flandreau, Marc, 2018. The other way: a narrative history of the Bank of France. In: Rodney Edvinsson, Tor Jacobson and Daniel Waldenström (eds.), *Sveriges Riksbank and the History of Central Banking*. Cambridge and New York: Cambridge University Press, 206–241.

Borges, José Ferreira, 1827. *Do Banco de Lisboa*. Lisboa: Tipografia de António Rodrigues Galhardo.

*Breve ensaio para servir à História do Banco de Lisboa*, 1828. Lisboa: Impressão Régia.

Caetano, António Alves, 2020. *Perfídia. Conde do Farrobo*. Lisboa: author's edition.

Costa, Cláudio Adriano, 1826. *Carta a S. Exª o Ministro da Fazenda sobre a extinção do papel-moeda*. Lisboa: Impressão Régia.

[*DC*] *Diário das Cortes Gerais e Extraordinárias da Nação Portuguesa* and *Diário da Câmara dos Senhores Deputados da Nação Portuguesa*. 1821–1822, 1822–1823 and 1826–1828. Lisboa: Impressão Régia.

Deleplace, Ghislain, 2013. The role of the standard in Ricardo's theory of money. In: Yugi Sato and Susumo Takenaga (eds.), *Ricardo on Money and Finance. A Bicentenary Reappraisal*. London and New York: Routledge, 115–123.

Diatkine, Sylvie, 2013. Interest rates, banking theory and monetary policy in Ricardo's economics. In: Yugi Sato and Susumo Takenaga (eds.), *Ricardo on Money and Finance. A bicentenary reappraisal*. London and New York: Routledge, 124–146.

Fetter, F. W. and Gregory, D., 1973. *Monetary and Financial Policy* (Series Government and Society in Nineteenth-Century Britain). London: Irish University Press.

Flandreau, Marc, 2021. What is in a bond? The value of Portugal or the financial origins of the Portuguese civil war. In: Luís Brites Pereira, Maria Eugénia Mata and Miguel Rocha de Sousa (eds.), *Economic Globalization and Governance. Essays in Honour of Jorge Braga de Macedo*. Cham: Springer, 35–50.

Fortune, Thomas, 1801. *História Breve e Autêntica do Banco de Inglaterra*. Lisboa: Tipografia do Arco do Cego (translation by Hipólito José da Costa).

Macedo, Jorge Borges, 1963. *Elementos para a História Bancária de Portugal, 1797–1820*. Lisboa: Instituto de Alta Cultura.

Matta, José Caeiro da, 1932–1933. O Banco de Portugal: esboço histórico. *Boletim do Banco de Portugal* (Serviço de Estatística e Estudos Económicos), nº 1, 5–30 e nº 2, 3–24.

Neal, Larry, 1990. *The Rise of Financial Capitalism. International Capital Markets in the Age of Reason*. Cambridge and New York: Cambridge University Press.

Neves, Maria Eugénia, 2013. O Banco de Lisboa. In: Faria, Miguel Figueira e Mendes, José Amado (coord.), *Dicionário de História Empresarial Portuguesa. Volume I. Instituições Bancárias*. Lisboa: Imprensa Nacional Casa da Moeda e Univ. Autónoma de Lisboa, 176–183.

Nunes, João Andrade, 2018. Contributo para um estudo histórico-jurídico do Banco de Lisboa. *Revista de Direito das Sociedades*, IX:1, 79–133.

O'Brien, Dennis P., 2004. *The Classical Economists Revisited*. Princeton: Princeton University Press (2nd revised edition).

O'Brien, Patrick and Palma, Nuno, 2020. Danger to the Old Lady of Threadneedle street? The Bank Restriction Act and the regime shift to paper money, 1797–1821. *European Review of Economic History*, 24:2, 390–426.

Pedreira, Jorge Miguel, 1995. *Os Homens de Negócio da Praça de Lisboa, de Pombal ao Vintismo (1755–1822). Diferenciação, Reprodução e Identificação de um Grupo Social*. Lisboa: FCSH/UNL (PhD dissertation).

Peres, Damião, 1971. *História do Banco de Portugal (1821–1846)*. Lisboa: Banco de Portugal.

Pohl, Manfred (ed.), 1994. *Handbook on the History of European Banks*. Aldershot: Edward Elgar.

*Regulamento do Banco de Lisboa precedido das leis, ofícios do Presidente da Assembleia Geral e Resolução das Cortes relativas ao mesmo Banco*, 1822. Lisboa: Tipografia Maigrense.

Reis, Jaime, 1996. *O Banco de Portugal. Das origens a 1914*. Lisboa: Banco de Portugal.

Reis, Jaime, 2010. "Popular capitalism" or plutocracy? The proprietorship of the Bank of Portugal, 1846–1914. In: J. Morilla, J. Hernández Andreu, J. L. García Ruiz e J. Mª. Ortiz-Villajos (Eds.), *Homenaje a Gabriel Tortella: las claves del desarrollo económico y social*. Madrid: Universidad de Alcalá, 663–684.

*Retrospecto sobre a administração do Banco de Lisboa e de Portugal: com algumas considerações análogas, oferecido à Assembleia Geral do Banco de Portugal em 1850 por um acionista*, 1850. Lisboa: Tipografia de Borges.

Ricardo, David, 1816. *Proposals for an Economical and Secure Currency*. In: *Works and Correspondence of David Ricardo*. Cambridge and New York: Cambridge University Press (edited by Piero Sraffa), Vol. IV, 43–141.

Robledo, Ricardo, 1988. Quienes eran los accionistas del Banco de España? *Revista de Historia Económica*, 6:3, 557–591.

Rosselli, Annalisa, 1999. The origin of the political economy of money. *Review of Political Economy*, 11:4, 443–454.

Soares, L. Ribeiro, 1971. *A Moeda em Portugal – breve história*. Lisboa: Banco de Portugal.

Tedde de Lorca, Pedro, 1999. Los primeros ciento cincuenta años del Banco de España (1782–1931). In: Pablo Martín Aceña y Manuel Titos Martínez (eds.), *El Sistema Financiero en España. Una síntesis histórica*. Granada: Universidad de Granada, 53–82.

Temin, Peter and Voth, Hans-Joachim, 2013. *Prometheus Shackled. Goldsmith Banks and England's Financial Revolution after 1700*. Oxford and New York: Oxford University Press.

Valério, Nuno (ed.), 2006. *História do Sistema Bancário Português*. Lisboa: Banco de Portugal, Vol I.

White, Lawrence H., 1984. *Free Banking in Britain. Theory, Experience, and Debate, 1800–1845*. Cambridge and New York: Cambridge University Press.

# 6 Concluding remarks

After the crisis of 1827, the Bank of Lisbon passed through a phase in which its activity was notably reduced and which lasted until the years of the Civil War of 1832–34. In the aftermath of this troubled period in Portuguese political life, the Bank of Lisbon recovered its position as the State's lending institution, shared the function of a bank of issue with the *Banco Comercial do Porto* (created in 1835), put in place a new programme for the extinction of paper money, benefited from the climate of political stability brought by the governments of Costa Cabral, at the beginning of the 1840s, and sponsored the creation of financial companies that were also intended to provide funds for the functioning of State services and the reorganisation of the public finance system. A new crisis was to occur in 1846, on the eve and in the context of fresh political and civil disturbances, which ended up dictating the expected institutional outcome of the restructuring of the banking and financial institutions that would lead to a merger between the Bank of Lisbon and the *Companhia Confiança Nacional*, as well as ultimately to the birth of the Bank of Portugal. But that is another story of reinvention and metamorphosis of an institution that, over a period of 25 years, effectively fulfilled the destiny established for it by the decision of the *Cortes Constituintes* that had emerged from the Liberal Revolution of 1820.

This study that is now coming to its conclusion has focused on the history of a banking institution during a precise phase of a much longer path of development. Although this is a focused, and therefore necessarily incomplete, history, it offers reasons for its being included in a broader spectrum of essays on the history of banking institutions and practices on a global scale.

Among the diversity of themes and perspectives offered by studies in banking history, one should point out, on the one hand, the analysis of the relationship between the organisation of banking systems and the processes of stable economic growth, and, on the other hand, the analysis of the role of banking crises in causing the negative phases of the business cycle (Colvin 2015; Grossman 2010). The role of banks in the issue of banknotes and the acceleration of monetary circulation, their place within the political system, especially in the definition and implementation of monetary policies, the instrumental nature of their economic functions in raising savings and investments, and their contribution to balancing the financial system, are all common generic features that

DOI: 10.4324/9781003355625-6

make banks indispensable for the stability of contemporary economies. It was at the beginning of the nineteenth century that this indispensability began to be clearly discerned.

This contribution towards the history of the early years of the Bank of Lisbon and its immediate antecedents allows us to illustrate, as a case study, some of the more general and common characteristics of the banking history of the period under analysis. However, the specificity of the Portuguese case suggests that special attention should be paid to the relationship between the banking organisation, the political process and the formation of the public sphere.

The creation of the Bank of Lisbon took place at a particularly fertile historical moment for the explanation of how economic circumstances, the political context and the public sphere interfered with the decision-making processes that justified its establishment at the end of 1821. The history of the Bank of Lisbon is an integral part of the history of the Portuguese liberal revolution and of the dismantling of the economic and financial system of the *ancien régime*.

The analysis of failed attempts to set up banks in the early years of the nineteenth century, as well as the unsuccessful experience of the creation of the Bank of Brazil in 1808 (serving the Portuguese court residing in Rio de Janeiro between 1808 and 1821), makes it possible to understand the essential features that the Bank of Lisbon displayed: a private bank created and protected by the legislative power with a mandate to issue banknotes for the purposes of regularising monetary circulation, and with the function of financing the State for current payments, as well as for the amortisation of the past public debt and the creation of future debt. Furthermore, the Bank of Lisbon also had the opportunity to develop other business areas that demonstrated, in the first years of its activity, how it was possible to reconcile the shareholders' own particular interests and the general interest supposedly represented by the State.

Its foundation was a process that was widely discussed and in which many people participated, giving rise to multiple testimonies about its vocation, and even providing theoretical debates about the great themes of that particular time: the public debt and fiduciary circulation. Since it was an institution funded by private capital, one might perhaps have expected greater independence and autonomy in the decision-making processes or in the definition of its privileged spheres of action. However, the aim of contributing to the re-establishment of public trust and credit conferred upon the Bank of Lisbon the status of a 'quasi-central bank' with the obligations of lending and issuing money. The fact that the Bank of Lisbon was a public bank with private capital did not prevent it from playing the role usually entrusted to a central monetary authority, which did not exist as such at the time.

Throughout the first years of its activity, between 1822 and 1828, the Bank of Lisbon did not entirely satisfy the first aspirations of doing away with the bad (paper) money that subverted the debt securities that it had ceased to represent. But it imposed itself as an indispensable instrument for the fulfilment of the financial obligations of the liberal State that was then under construction.

I hope that the readers have appreciated the relevance of this historical case study devoted to the early beginnings of the banking system in Portugal. Not only because of the new approach that it offers to the history of the Bank of Lisbon, but also because it illustrates wider problems of a universal nature and invites us to establish present-day parallels linking the importance of monetary and financial institutions to the political environment and consequent policy implications.

The history of the establishment of the Bank of Lisbon thus provides an excellent opportunity for the further discussion of the present and future problems of an economic nature that are related to banking practices: public debt management; the imbalances and inflationary effects of an excess money supply; rules versus discretion in monetary policy; prudential concerns regarding the outcome of banking activities; the independence of banking institutions *vis-à-vis* state control and regulation; the expectations of economic agents about the banks' capacity to fulfil their current requirements; incentives and instruments to promote investment and economic growth; public confidence in the credit system; the reputational risk associated with bad management; tensions between private interests and the common good. These are all issues that stem from the narrative about banking and politics in the early nineteenth century, thus confirming the merits of historical approaches for providing a better understanding of the world we live in.

## References

Colvin, Christopher, 2015. The past, present and future of banking history. *QUCEH Working Papers Series*, WP 2015/05.

Grossman, Richard S., 2010. *Unsettled Account: The Evolution of Banking in the Industrialized World since 1800*. Princeton: Princeton University Press.

# Appendix

## Legal charter for the creation of the Bank of Lisbon, 31 December 1821

Transcription of the *Regulations of the Bank of Lisbon preceded by the laws, official letters of the President of the General Meeting and the Decision of Parliament relating to the same Bank*. Lisbon: Tipografia Maigrense, 1822.

I, Dom João, by the Grace of God and by the Constitution of the Monarchy, King of the United Kingdom of Portugal, Brazil, and the Algarves, the Overseas in Africa, etc., make it known to all my subjects that the Parliament has decreed as follows:

Taking into consideration the public advantage that results from the establishment of a bank for the lending, deposit and discounting of money, which, by exiling usury and promoting the convenience of transactions between private citizens, is simultaneously applicable to the amortisation of paper money, the General, Extraordinary and Constituent Parliament of the Portuguese Nation decrees as follows:

1. A corporation shall be established in the city of Lisbon, with the name of the Bank of Lisbon, which will exist for a period of twenty years, under the immediate protection of the Parliament.
2. Its capital shall be composed of ten thousand shares, each with the value of five hundred thousand *réis*, paid in equal sums of paper money and specie.
3. The subscription to this bank shall open on the first of January of eighteen hundred and twenty-two, under the supervision of three persons, appointed by the President of the Parliament; and, as soon as it amounts to two thousand five hundred *contos de réis*, one hundred and fifty of the subscribers who have subscribed to the largest number of shares, shall form the General Meeting of the bank and shall appoint, by the largest numbers of votes, a President, and sixteen Directors, each of whom shall be Portuguese by birth or though naturalisation; and furthermore the owner of at least twelve shares.
4. The General Meeting shall decide upon the salaries of the President, and Directors, and these will appoint the staff necessary to ensure the bank's services; their salaries will, however, be established by the Meeting, which will also designate the day and place, upon which the bank will begin its

operations; and it will establish a set of Regulations for its administration, and bookkeeping, and whose doctrine is in accordance with the existing laws, and the provisions of the present decree.

5. Once the Regulations have been completed, and the administration of the bank has been delivered to the President, and Directors, the General Meeting shall be dissolved.
6. A General Meeting, composed of the one hundred and fifty main shareholders, shall be held each year in the month of January in order to elect the President, and Directors; to take knowledge of and consider the accounts of the previous year; to correct the abuses that have been introduced into the administration; and to request improvements from the Parliament, which will depend upon the legislative body. The General Meeting may also be convened extraordinarily before the end of the year, if it is necessary to deliberate on unforeseen cases, which the Directors are not sufficiently authorised to decide upon for themselves.
7. The General Assembly, and the Directors of the Bank, through their Presidents, shall have the power to correspond directly with the Parliament.
8. The bank may discount and negotiate bills of exchange, and all credit documents that are used in trade, being guaranteed by the number and quality of signatures, as established in its Regulations; the assets of the acceptors and guarantors will be tacitly and specially mortgaged to the payment thereof. This mortgage does not, however, prejudice the laws that regulate contests in the event of the bankruptcy of the dealers.
9. It may lend its funds against all manner of goods, merchandise and movable property, which it will receive as a deposit; and, should the debtor not pay within the appointed time, it may on his account, without the need for his consent, proceed to sell the deposited pledge by auction, publicly announcing this sale eight days beforehand.
10. In its loans, it may receive property as a mortgage, with the explanations and guarantees that it considers appropriate, and proceed to the sale thereof when payment is not made at the end of the loan period, as if it were its own property, preceded by a public announcement thirty days prior to the act of sale.
11. It may buy and sell paper money, and all of the nation's other credit certificates, as well as gold, and silver, in any form, kind or quality.
12. It may keep the money deposited by private citizens, with which it will open a current account, and on whose orders it will pay on demand the part of the sums deposited when it is requested to do so.
13. It may also receive from private citizens, to be paid at fixed times, in return for a stipulated annual interest, the sums of money that it considers opportune for increasing its operations.
14. The bank will not pay any tax or contribution on all these negotiations, loans and transactions.

15. The bank may not undertake any business involving risk, or insurance, nor buy or sell commercial goods on its own behalf, just as it may not own any property other than the urban buildings that are necessary for the performance of its operations.
16. It also may not confirm or agree any loan with the government without the prior consent of the Parliament, nor may the same government have any involvement in the management thereof.
17. In order to promote their circulation, the bank may issue a quantity of banknotes, payable to the bearer in specie, or bills on demand, with some days being needed for their clearance, for the comfort of travellers. And this issue of both banknotes and bills of exchange shall be made in such proportions that it will never expose the bank to the need to defer or interrupt its payments.
18. The banknotes will be received and considered in all the departments of the Public Treasury as specie; but the State's creditors will not be obliged to receive these notes in payment of their loans.
19. Those who falsify in any way papers belonging to the bank shall be prosecuted and tried as counterfeiters.
20. The bank's shares may be sold, donated, transferred or mortgaged, with the respective amounts being recorded for this purpose in the bank's ledgers.
21. The shares, profits or funds that exist at the bank, belonging to foreigners, shall, in all cases, even in war, be as inviolable and respected as Portuguese property.
22. Every six months, the product of the net profit will be divided among the shareholders. However, when this profit exceeds the rate of seven per cent per year, the General Meeting may convert the excess into reserve funds, with the conditions that it considers appropriate.
23. During the twenty years of the bank's existence, no other corporation will be created in Portugal with the privileges that are granted to this one.
24. In compensation for the prerogatives that the nation grants to the bank, the latter shall contribute to the amortisation of paper money, lending the nation, in the first year of its operations, two thousand *contos de réis* in banknotes at 4 per cent interest, delivered to the National Treasury in twenty instalments of one hundred *contos de réis* each.
25. When the Treasury receives each of these instalments, it will, in the presence of the bank's agents, and of private citizens wishing to attend this act, amortise an equal nominal amount of paper money; printing and subsequently publishing a list with an individual explanation of the class, year and number of the destroyed securities.
26. In the act of receiving the instalment, the Treasury shall deliver to the bank a debt certificate that will, from the day of its delivery, bear an interest of four per cent per year, paid in specie every six months by the second coffer of the Board of Interest: from the first of January of eighteen hundred and twenty-two, the revenue thereof, increased with a third of the annual

product of the fifth coffer, will be exclusively used firstly for the payment of this interest and its capital, and then for the extinction of paper money.

27. By virtue of this loan, and without altering the form of its revenue, the National Treasury will pay during one year in paper money only the fourth part of all the amounts that it customarily paid in accordance with the law.
28. When the Public Treasury begins to pay only the fourth part in paper money, three per cent in metal money will be discounted from the total of each payment, in which paper money is normally used, made at the different offices that receive money from the same Treasury. In those offices, however, that, because they are public, do not receive money from the Treasury, the said discount will be only two per cent; and in each of the two cases, the same discount will be made for all twenty years of the bank's existence.
29. The amounts resulting from the three and two per cent, discounted in accordance with the preceding clause, will be collected at the different offices and kept in a separate safe, and sent each month to the Board of Interest, where they will be stored in the coffer intended for the amortisation of the bank's debt.
30. Through this coffer, one of the certificates of the debt that the nation has taken out with the bank will be amortised each year, according to their length of existence, and under the terms of article twenty-six.
31. Before the end of the first year of the bank's establishment, in accordance with the credit that exists in the form of paper money and the sum that exists in the amortisation fund, the Parliament will decide whether it is convenient to take out another loan, arranged under new terms, in order to continue the amortisation by this, or any other, method, and will establish the quantity of paper money that must enter into the payments which the National Treasury will make the following year.
32. In order to prevent the falsification to which the current paper money is subject, during the time that it still remains in circulation, the government is authorised to make the necessary expenditure, should it consider it convenient to do so, in order to obtain and use the printing plates invented by the famous artist Perkins for the formation of a new paper money that will replace the old one.

Paço das Cortes on the twenty-ninth of December eighteen hundred and twenty-one.

Accordingly, I instruct all the authorities responsible for the knowledge and execution of the aforesaid decree to fulfil and execute it in full. Issued at Paço de Queluz on the thirty-first day of the month of December 1821.

On behalf of the King
José Inácio da Costa

*Legal Charter, whereby Your Majesty orders the execution of the decree of the General, Extraordinary and Constituent Parliament of the Portuguese Nation, for the establishment of a corporation, by the name of the* Bank of Lisbon, *for the lending, deposit and discounting of money, which, by exiling usury and promoting the convenience of transactions between private citizens, is simultaneously applicable to the amortisation of paper money, with a lifetime of twenty years, composed of capital consisting of ten thousand shares, each with the value of five hundred thousand* réis, *under the terms of the law; whose subscription will be opened on the first of January of the future year of eighteen hundred and twenty-two, all in the manner described above.*

For Your Majesty to see.

# Index